CONGRESSIONAL CLUB
Recipes

WILDSIDE PRESS

Contents

	Page
Editorial Pages	4
Appetizers, Sandwiches and Beverages	7
Breads	27
Cake, Cookies and Candies	67
Desserts	119
Favorite Dishes Served at the Club	159
Fish and Fowl	171
Meat and Luncheon Dishes	211
Pastry	265
Pickels and Preserves	269
Salads, Dressings and Sauces	301
Soups	337
Vegetables	353

Editorial Pages

	Page
Contents	3
Club Officers	5
Club Recipes Committee — Mrs. Lawrence Smith	6
Dedication — Mrs. Hal Holmes	381
Household Hints	385
Index	395
Notes	391

Congressional Club Officers

1945 — 1947

President
Mrs. Harold H. Burton, Ohio

Vice-Presidents
Mrs. Emmet O'Neal, Kentucky
Mrs. W. Sterling Cole, New York
Mrs. J. Buell Snyder, Pennsylvania
Mrs. Clinton P. Anderson, New Mexico
Mrs. Frank A. Barrett, Wyoming

Recording Secretary
Mrs. Robert L. F. Sikes, Florida

Corresponding Secretary
Mrs. Thomas E. Martin, Iowa

Treasurer
Mrs. Everett M. Dirksen, Illinois

~ Club Recipes Committee ~

Mrs. Lawrence H. Smith, Wisconsin, Chairman
Mrs. Sherman Adams, New Hampshire
Mrs. Frank A. Barrett, Wyoming
Mrs. C. W. Bishop, Illinois
Mrs. Henry C. Dworshak, Idaho
Mrs. Clarence E. Hancock, New York
Mrs. Hal Holmes, Washington
Mrs. Robert R. Rich, Pennsylvania
Mrs. Karl Stefan, Nebraska
Mrs. Frank L. Sundstrom, New Jersey
Mrs. Dean P. Taylor, New York

♪ THANK YOU NOTE ♪
"my thanks, committee, here appears." "Thank you, very much, my dears."
♪ Eleanor Smith

Appetizers
Sandwiches
Beverages

Index of Appetizers

Canapes	9, 10
Cheese Rolls (Hors d'oeuvres)	11
Fruit Butterball	12
Frozen Tomato Juice Cocktail	13
Hawaiian Cocktails	14
Strawberry and Pear Cocktail	15

Sandwiches

Cinnamon Toast	16
Crab filling for sandwichs	17
Frosted Sandwich Loaf	18
Lunch box Sandwich Fillings	19
Sandwich Fillings	20
Toasted Tuna Fish Sandwich	21

Beverages

Bohemian Tea	22
Hot Wassail	23
Mint Cocktail	24
Swedish Christmas Tea	25

Canapes

Raw cauliflower flowerlets and tiny cherry tomatoes, canned artichoke hearts, cooked shrimp, cooked small beets, arranged on a platter around a bowl of Russian dressing make a refreshing cold canapé.

Russian Dressing

1/2 cup mayonnaise dressing
1/4 cup chili sauce
1 tsp. Worchestershire sauce
1 T. lemon juice
1/4 tsp. Tobasco sauce or pinch of Cayenne pepper

Mrs. Clarence Hancock
New York

Canapes

Paprika Sticks

Cut each slice Pullman Bread into 5 fingers.
Toast in slow oven until crisp & slightly colored.
Brush with melted butter colored with paprika.
Cool - decorate with Ribbon Roquefort spread.
Serve with cocktail course.

Chipped Beef Canape

Spread chipped beef with mixture cream
cheese & horseradish. Roll & chill.
Cut in suitable lengths & serve on toothpicks

Horn's Point Special

Chopped Chives. 1 cake cream cheese
1 T. Roquefort cheese. 1 T. Sherry or Maderia
1 t. Worcestershire sauce
1 T. butter — salt.
Mix & chill. Spread on toast or crackers.

Mrs. Jae Kendricks
Florida

Cheese Rolls (Hors d'oeuvres)

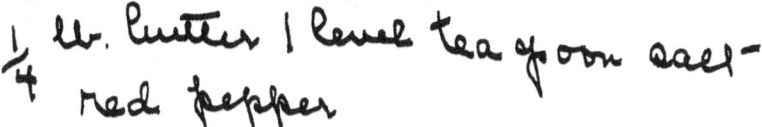

1 lb. cheese grated
2 cups plain flour
1/2 lb. black walnut meats
1/4 lb. butter 1 level teaspoon salt — red pepper

Knead lightly until smooth. Roll out on a lightly floured board in 1/4 inch thickness. Sprinkle and pat in nut-meats. Roll up like a jelly roll. Wrap in waxed paper and place in refrigerator until firm.

Slice and bake in a moderate oven.

Mrs. William A. Burgin
North Carolina

Fruit Butterball

Combine - 1 C. mashed Avocado
1 tsp. grated onion
1½ tsp. lemon juice
Few drops Tabasco Sauce
Salt to taste

Whip until smooth.
A good spread for hot bread or on toast for canape's.

Mrs John M Robison
Kentucky

Frozen Tomato Juice Cocktail

5 C. tomato juice
1 T. horseradish
2 T. minced green pepper
3 T.   "   celery
1 tsp salt
4 tsp lemon juice
4 tsp tarragon vinegar
¼ tsp tabasco

Mix + freeze to mushy stage

Serve in cocktail glasses with topping of ¼ tsp. mayonnaise to 1 T. whipped cream.

Good served with paprika sticks.

Mrs Sid Simpson
Illinois

Hawaiian Cocktails
Sauce

1/4 C. chili sauce
1 tsp. Worcestershire Sauce
1 T lemon juice
1 T. mayonnaise
1/4 tsp. salt

Avocado cocktail –

1 large avocado, chilled, pared + cubed
Arrange in glasses + top each with sauce.

Cucumber cocktail –

Peel and cut cucumbers in small squares. Boil until tender in salted water. Chill and serve in sauce.

Mrs. Joseph Rider Farrington
Hawaii

Strawberry & Pear Cocktail

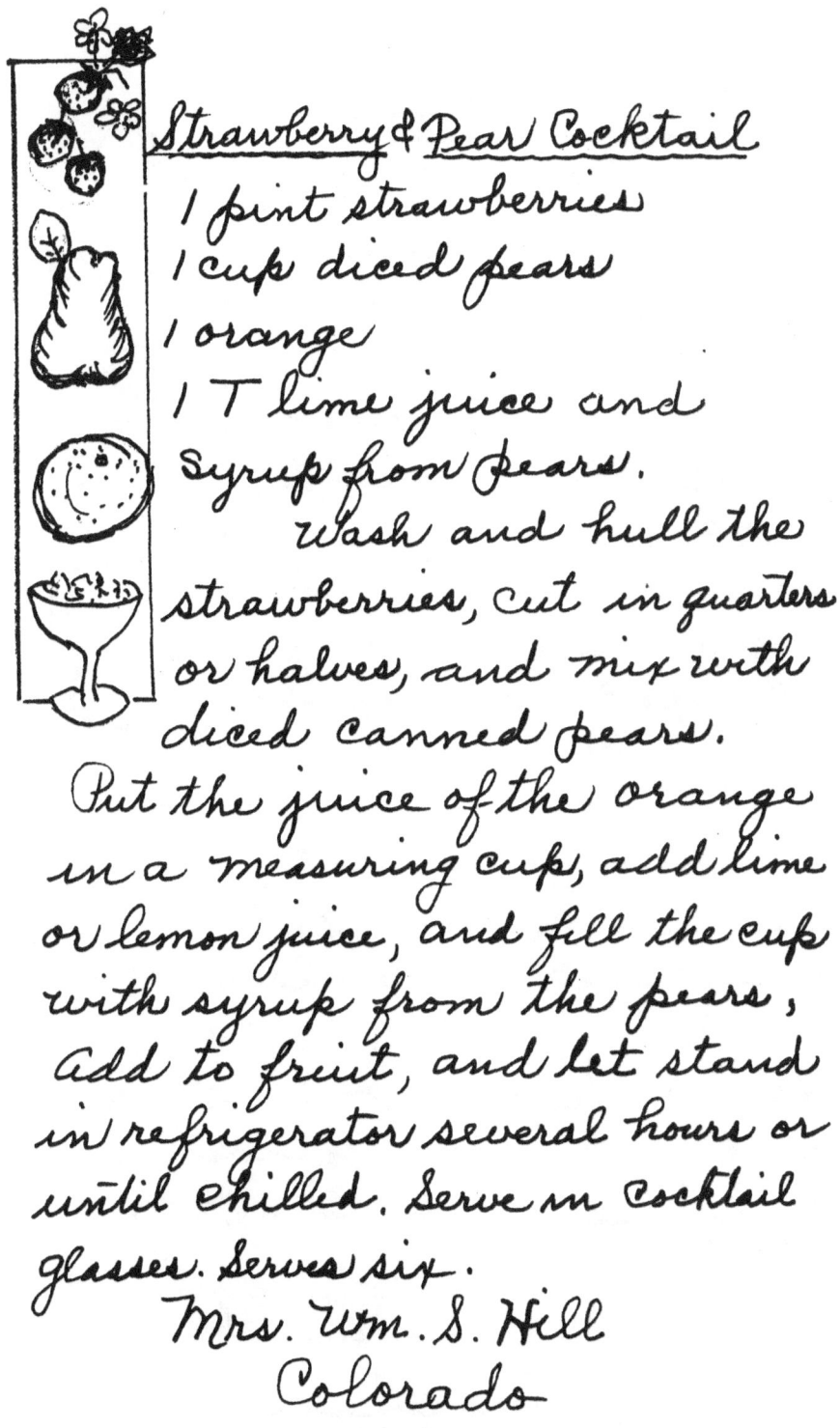

1 pint strawberries
1 cup diced pears
1 orange
1 T lime juice and syrup from pears.

Wash and hull the strawberries, cut in quarters or halves, and mix with diced canned pears. Put the juice of the orange in a measuring cup, add lime or lemon juice, and fill the cup with syrup from the pears. Add to fruit, and let stand in refrigerator several hours or until chilled. Serve in cocktail glasses. Serves six.

Mrs. Wm. S. Hill
Colorado

Cinnamon Toast

½ Cube butter or enough to absorb 6 T. Confectioners sugar and 2 T. Cinnamon. Melt the butter slowly, add sugar and cinnamon and about 2 T. finely chopped walnuts. Toast bread on one side, turn over and spread generously with cinnamon mixture. Place under broiler till it bubbles, (take care not to burn it). It is different from most cinnamon toast — serve for tea.

   Mrs Laurence Smith
    Wisconsin

Crab filling for Sandwiches.

Remove all pieces of shell from Crab meat.

Add mayonnaise and small amount of horse radish.

A little grated onion may be added if desired.

Mix well making paste.

Mrs. Edward Everett Gunn
Kansas

Frosted Sandwich Loaf

1 loaf sandwich bread
2 pkgs. Philadelphia cream cheese
Butter or margarine
Fillings - 1. egg salad
  2. Sardine or fish salad
  3. Chopped cucumber + water cress
  4. Chopped dates, apricots or prunes
  5. Chopped nut meats
or other preferred spread — not too moist.

Remove crust from bread + slice lengthwise in thick slices. Butter both sides of slices. Spread each slice with a filling + form layers. Press firmly together. Wrap tightly in wax paper + chill in ice box for several hours.

Cream the cheese + moisten enough to make a stiff spread. Frost the loaf with cheese + sprinkle with chopped nuts. Chill at least 1 hour + slice for serving.

Elizabeth Michener Quick
Michigan

Lunch Box Sandwich Fillings

I. Grind hard cooked eggs, add chopped bacon and mayonnaise. Substitute for bacon, ham, Spam or cold cuts.

II. Crab, lobster, shrimp or any white fish-mashed. Season with lemon juice, cayenne + mayonnaise.

III. Peanut butter, chopped bacon + relish.

IV. Cream cheese, orange marmalade, nuts + cream to make moist.

V. Mash cold baked beans to a paste. Season with chopped celery and prepared mustard.

VI. Cottage cheese, minced chipped beef and chopped chives.

VII. Hard cooked eggs-chopped fine - salt, pepper, curry powder + mayonnaise. Celery seeds are good substitute for curry.

VIII. Ground ham or other meat, sour pickles, a little horseradish and mayonnaise.

IX. Cream cheese combined with chopped nut meats, chopped stuffed olives, chopped red or green peppers or finely sliced preserved ginger.

X. Chopped dates or figs, nut meats and mayonnaise.

Mrs Walt. Horan
Washington

— Sandwich Fillings —

I. Can of sardines
   1/4 C grated "rat" cheese   } Mash into paste.
   1/2 chopped onion
   Let blend 4 or 5 hrs. before

II. Mashed hard boiled eggs Moisten with soft butter. Season with anchovy.

III. 1 T. Indian Chutney   Few grains cayenne
    2 chopped pickles   1/4 tsp. salt
    1 T Worcestershire Sauce
    Mix well into 4 oz. cream cheese

IV. Hard boiled eggs - chopped. Add curry powder, salt, pepper + mayonnaise.

V. For open sandwich — Grind in meat chopper 2 pickles, 2 anchovies, 2 hard cooked egg yolks, 1 sprig parsley + 3 T capers. Mix in 2 T olive oil, 2 T. vinegar, 1 tsp. prepared mustard, salt + paprika. Spread on bread. Cut in fancy shapes. Top with chopped egg whites.

Mrs. Jerry Vonhio   California

Toasted Tuna Fish Sandwich

1 can tuna fish
1 T lemon juice
1/4 tsp salt
Dash of cayenne
1/2 C. mayonnaise
8 slices toasted bread

2 T. anchovy paste
2 T. butter
1/2 head lettuce
1 large tomato
8 ripe olives
2 dill pickles

Drain can of tuna. Mix with lemon juice, salt, cayenne + mayonnaise. Cream anchovy paste + butter, spread on toast. Spread tuna mixture on 4 pieces of toast, cover with remaining slices. Garnish with lettuce, tomato, olives and sliced pickles.

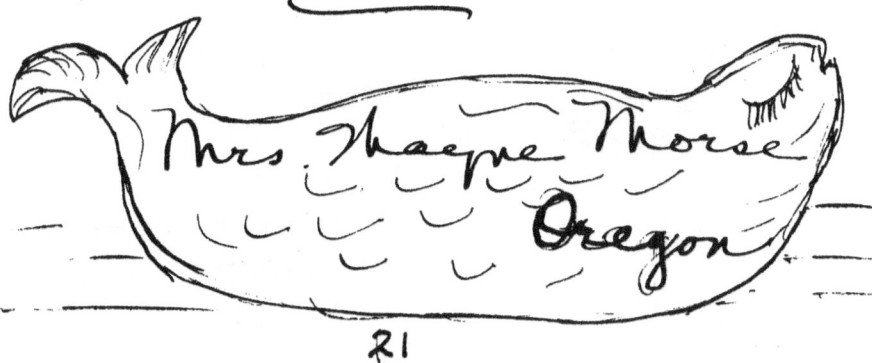

Mrs. Wayne Morse
Oregon

BOHEMIAN TEA

Pour 2 c. boiling water over 2 t. black tea and rind of 3 lemons. Steep 15 minutes. Strain and pour hot over 1½ c. sugar and juice of 3 lemons. Keep in icebox. To serve take 1 part syrup to 3 water. Add plenty of ice!

Mrs. Howard Buffett
Nebraska

Hot Wassail
(A delicious drink for a winter night!)

2 oranges } squeeze and reserve
2 lemons } the juice

2 sticks cinnamon } Simmer together
2 T whole (or ground) } (tightly covered)
  cloves (or allspice) } with the squeezed
1 C sugar } orange and lemon
1½ qts. water } halves, for one
             } hour, or more.

Strain —
Add one gallon fresh apple cider and the reserved orange and lemon juice —
Reheat and serve hot.

Mrs. Walter H. Judd
Minnesota

Mint Cocktail

Pulp of 3 oranges

1 no. 2 can pineapple diced

¼ lb. after dinner mints

Mix, chill one hour and serve with crushed ice.

Mrs. John S. Wood — Georgia

Swedish Christmas Tea

To one quart of freshly made strong tea, add 1 qt. best grape juice, and juice of one lemon.

Place the following in a small bag:
Yellow rind of one lemon (avoid white!)
½ dozen cloves (discard soft part of head)
¼ tsp. grated nutmeg,
½ inch cinnamon stick,
2 dozen cardamon seed (from drug store) rolled fine.

Add this bag to kettle containing the tea and juices.
Simmer 3 hours, with vessel tightly closed.
Sweeten to taste (2 to 3 rounded T sugar)
N.B. Swedes add a dash of rum.

Serve hot with small Christmas cakes or cookies.
Quaint cups and plates enhance the effect.

— Mrs Martin A. Morrison
Indiana.

 # NOTES

Breads
Muffins
Hot Rolls

Breads

Bran Rolls	30
All Bran Rolls	31
Banana Bread	32
Buttermilk Biscuit	33
Cheese Biscuits	34
Cheese Cookies	35
Coffee Cake	36
Date and Nut Breads	37, 38
Drop Biscuits	39
Easy Ice Box Rolls	40, 41
Economy Biscuits	42
Excellent Substitute for Rolls	43
Gingerbread	44
Gooey Rolls	45
Graham Bread	46
Grapenut Bread	47
Hushpuppies	48
Ice Box Rolls	49
Kentucky Corn Cakes	50
Maryland Beaten Biscuit	51
Muffins	52
Pancakes (Nalesniki)	53
Pecan Rolls	54
Refrigerator Rolls	55, 56

Rolls	57
Sally Lunn Muffins	58
Scotch Scones	59
Southern Spoon Bread	60
Spoon Bread	61
Swedish Biscuits	62
Waffles	63, 64
Western Gold Waffles	65
West Virginia Spoon Bread	66

Bran Rolls —

Mix:
 ½ cup sugar
 ⅔ cup shortening
 1 cup all bran
 2 teaspoons salt

Pour over this 1 cup boiling water. Stir until dissolved.
Cool, then add 2 eggs beaten slightly, 2 cakes yeast dissolved in 1 cup warm water.
Add 7 cups flour.
Put in refrigerator.
Make out two hours before using.
Bake 15-20 minutes at 400°.

Bess W. Truman

All Bran Rolls

½ C. Shortening
½ C. boiling water
6 T. Sugar
½ C. Kellogs AllBran
Salt

} Combine and cool

1 egg - well beaten
1 cake yeast - dissolve in ½ c. water.

3 C. Flour
Combine mixtures 1 and 2. Add flour gradually, beating well. Knead dough lightly. Roll dough to about ½ inch thickness; Cut as for Parker House Rolls. For variety I make Clover leaf Rolls. Dough keeps well in refrigerator several days.

Let stand 2 hours - Bake.

Mrs. George B. Schwabe
Oklahoma

Banana Bread

1 cup sugar
½ cup Crisco
2 eggs – well beaten
3 mashed bananas
8 T cold water
2 ½ cups flour
1 t. soda
1 cup nut meats
1 t. baking powder.

Sift dry ingredients and add to other mixture. Bake in slow oven 1 hr.

Mrs. Reid Murray
Wisconsin

Buttermilk Biscuit

2 C. flour
1 c buttermilk
4 T shortening
1 t salt
½ t soda

Into the flour put salt, soda and sift into bowl. Mix in shortening with tips of fingers or chop in with spoon and make into dough. Lift onto a well floured board, knead just to get firm enough to roll. Roll out to ½ inch thick, cut and place on baking sheet. Bake in hot oven ten minutes.

Mrs. Malcolm C. Tower
Georgia.

Cheese Biscuit

2 C of grated cheese
1 C of soft butter
About 4 C of flour
Salt & pepper to taste
Cream butter & cheese, add
salt & pepper.
Add flour & work with
hands until about the
consistency of tea cake
dough. Chill, roll out
½ in. thick, cut with
small biscuit cutter &
bake in hot oven
until brown.

Mrs. Stephen Pace
Georgia

Cheese Cookies

1 C grated cheese

1 C. butter (or substitute)

1 C. flour

Salt & red pepper to taste

Make stiff dough wrap in waxed paper store in ice box 'till needed, slice & bake

Mrs Walter F. George
Georgia

Coffee Cake

2 C flour
4 tsp baking powder
1/2 tsp salt
4 T brown sugar
4 T shortening
1 egg - beaten
1/2 C. milk
1/4 C. raisins

Topping
1 T melted butter 2 T sugar
1 tsp cinnamon

Sift flour, measure, sift with baking powder and salt. Add brown sugar - cut in shortening. Add egg, milk and raisins. Spread in oiled pan. Cover with topping. Bake 425° 20-25 minutes.

Mrs. Albert M. Cole
Kansas

Date and Nut Bread

½ C. sugar
1 egg
1 C. milk
½ tsp. salt
{ 2 C. flour (white)   } sift
{ 3 level tsp. baking powder } together.
1 C. walnut meats – chopped into small pieces.
1 C. dates – cut into small pieces and stewed in very little water.

Mix thoroughly. Bake 1 hour in greased bread pan. Slow oven.

Mrs. Charles F. McLaughlin
Nebraska

Date-Nut Bread

1 cup sugar
2 Tbl. spoons butter
1 egg
1 cup boiling water
1 tea spoon baking powder
1 cup nuts (pecans)
2½ cups flour
1 tea spoon soda
1 cup dates (chopped)

Method: Soak dates, boiling water and soda for few minutes add creamed sugar and butter and well beaten egg. Add flour and baking powder and nuts and bake in greased loaf pan for 30 minutes in moderate oven - (350°)

    Mrs Orville Zimmerman
          Missouri

Drop Biscuit

2 cups of flour
1 tablespoon of lard and butter
1 salt spoon of salt
1 large teaspoon of baking powder
1 large spoon of sugar
1 cup of milk

Rub lard and butter together, rub well into the flour — add sugar, stir in milk with a spoon, making stiffest kind of batter or softest kind of dough. Take paste on end of spoon, drop in little mounds on a greased pan. This takes 15 minutes to make and bake.

Mrs. Anderson H. Walters
of Pennsylvania

Easy Ice Box Rolls

½ C. fat
4 T. sugar } Cream well

1 egg, unbeaten, add to above

1 yeast cake
1 tbsp. sugar
4 T. warm water } Crumble yeast cake in water with sugar, to dissolve

1 C. warm water
4 C. flour
1½ tsp. salt } mix

Add wet and dry ingredients to fat mixture, and let stand in ice box at least 1 hour, as dough is very stiff.

40

Remove and beat air out of dough. (DO not knead).

Turn out on a well-floured board and pat top with flour. Cut with floured biscuit cutter or form cloverleaf rolls with 3 small balls of dough. Put in greased muffin pans; butter tops; cover and let rise 1 hour in warm place.
Bake about 15 min. at 400°.

Mrs. Finis J. Garrett
Tennessee

Economy Biscuits

1⅔ C. flour
3 H. tsps B.P.
½ tsps salt
¼ tsps sugar
⅓ C. shaved suet
⅔ C. milk

Mix shaved suet with sifted dry ingredients. Add milk, mix lightly. Drop from spoon into hot greased muffin pans. Bake at 350°-400° 12-15 minutes.

* Use instead of crust on meat pie.
* Add 1 Tbsp. for shortcake.

Mrs Karl Stefan
Nebraska.

Excellent Substitute Rolls

1 Loaf Unsliced Bread
½ C. Butter or Substitute

Cut crust from the top, sides, and end of loaf three fourths of the way down. Thin cut loaf in thirds or fourths lengthwise almost to bottom then across in suitable roll-size portions as before. Place in pan lined with wax paper and dribble melted butter over loaf. Brown slightly in hot oven. Serve whole from tray, each diner breaking off portion. Variation: Add garlic salt to butter.

Mrs. H. C. Dwoyshek,
—Idaho

Gingerbread

½ C. shortening
½ C. sugar
1 egg
1 tsp. ginger
1 tsp. cinnamon
1 tsp. soda

1½ C. flour
½ C. molasses
½ C. coffee (cold)

Cream together shortening and sugar, add beaten egg. Sift dry ingredients together, add alternately to mixture with molasses and coffee.

Mrs. John W. Heselton
Massachusetts

Gooey Rolls

Combine 3/4 C. milk, 1 tbsp. sugar, 1/2 tsp. salt and 3 tbsp. shortening - heat in sauce pan until the shortening is melted. Remove from stove and when luke-warm add 1 yeast cake and 1 beaten egg - mix well. Add enough flour to make a stiff dough. Knead lightly and place in greased bowl - let rise until double in bulk. (about 1 hr.) Place on floured board - Knead lightly and then roll to 1/2" thickness. Spread with butter & brown sugar - roll dough up (as for jelly roll) and slice off rolls of 1" thickness. Place in tins which have been prepared in the following manner and allow to rise until double in bulk - Grease tins with butter - sprinkle well with brown sugar and pecan meats - and pour over all a thin layer of Maple Syrup. Bake about 25 min.

Mrs. Sherman Adams
New Hampshire

~ Graham Bread ~

1 egg   Salt
1 C. Sour milk   1 Tsp. Soda
1 C. white flour   1 C. Graham flour
1/4 C. molasses   1 tbsp. Sugar

Mix and pour into greased bread tin. Bake in moderate oven about 45 minutes. Nuts or raisins may be added. Serve hot or cold.

Mrs. Sherman Adams
New Hampshire

Grapenut Bread

3/4 Cups grapenuts
1/2 Cup sugar – brown is best
1/2 tsp. soda
1 Cup sour milk – or buttermilk
mix to-gether and let stand 1/2 hour
Then add:
1 egg beaten
1 1/2 cups flour
1 tsp. baking powder
Put in bread tin and let stand
1 hour. Bake in 350° oven
about 35 minutes.

Mrs. Dudley A. White
Ohio

Hushpuppies

The perfect accompaniment to fried fish — an indispensible part of creek bank fish suppers in the deep South — came to us from pioneer camp fires.

1 c. corn meal
1 medium onion — chopped fine
1 tsp. Baking Powder
1 tsp. salt
3/4 c. water — approximately

Sift corn meal, salt & baking powder together. Add chopped onion, then water to make a stiff batter. Use a spoon to drop small patties into hot grease left from frying fish. Fry to a golden brown.

Mrs. Robert L. F. Sikes
Florida

48

Ice Box Rolls

Scald one quart sweet milk, cool to luke warm add one Fleischman's yeast cake, 1 cup sugar, 1 cup lard, & enough flour to make a light batter. Let rise 2 hours. Add 1 Tablespoon salt, light teaspoon soda, heaping teaspoon baking powder, enough flour to make stiff dough, put in ice box until ready to use, make out two hours before time to cook. Make into rolls, grease with butter let rise two hours.

Mrs John Rankin
49 Mississippi

Kentucky Corn Cakes

Delicious and lacy-edged are these corn cakes.

Ingredients:
Buttermilk — 1 pint
Soda — 1 level teaspoon
1 or 2 eggs
Corn meal
Salt

Add soda to buttermilk Cornmeal to make thin batter — egg — salt. Mix thoroughly, drop on hot greased griddle brown on both sides serve with lots of butter. A slice of "Old" Kentucky Ham fried a rich brown is a nice accompaniment.

There are other uses of corn in Kentucky.

Glessie M. O'Neal
(Mrs. Emmet O'Neal)
Louisville, Kentucky

Maryland Beaten Biscuit

6 Cups flour - finely bolted
1 Cup lard
1 teaspoon baking powder
1 teaspoon salt
All measurements level

Mix lard through flour with salt and baking powder. Add cold water to make a stiff dough. Beat with axe ½ hr. Make out into round biscuits. Flatten just a little and prick the top with a fork. Bake 25 minutes in a quick oven. Makes 3½ dozen.

Mrs. Dudley G. Roe
Maryland.

Muffins.

3 cups flour
3 teaspoons (level) baking powder
1 egg
½ teaspoon salt
Milk.

Light your oven; grease muffin pans with butter, beef grease or lard and put pans to warm. Beat ingredients together thoro'ly adding milk to make firm batter. Half fill muffin pans and pop in moderate oven 15 minutes.

Variations: add 2 tablespoons ground nuts, or orange juice, or crushed banana, or raisins.

Mrs. John C. Schafer
Wisconsin

Pancakes (Naleśniki)

4 eggs separated 2 C. milk
1/2 tsp. shortening 1/2 tsp. salt
1 C. flour 1 T. sugar
cheese filling

Combine beaten egg yolks, melted shortening, salt, sugar, milk and flour. Beat with an egg beater until smooth. Add stiffly beaten whites last. Fry on a griddle or frying pan until lightly browned on both sides. Cakes must be very thin. Spread with prepared cheese and fold like an envelope or roll. Fry again for added crispness on both sides, or put in the oven to heat thru, and serve sprinkled with powdered sugar or syrup.

Cheese filling

2 C. cottage cheese 2 T. milk
1 egg or 2 yolks beaten 2 T. sugar
1/2 tsp. salt

Combine well. Use as directed above. Raisins or currents may be added.

Mrs. Thomas S. Gordon
Illinois

Pecan Rolls

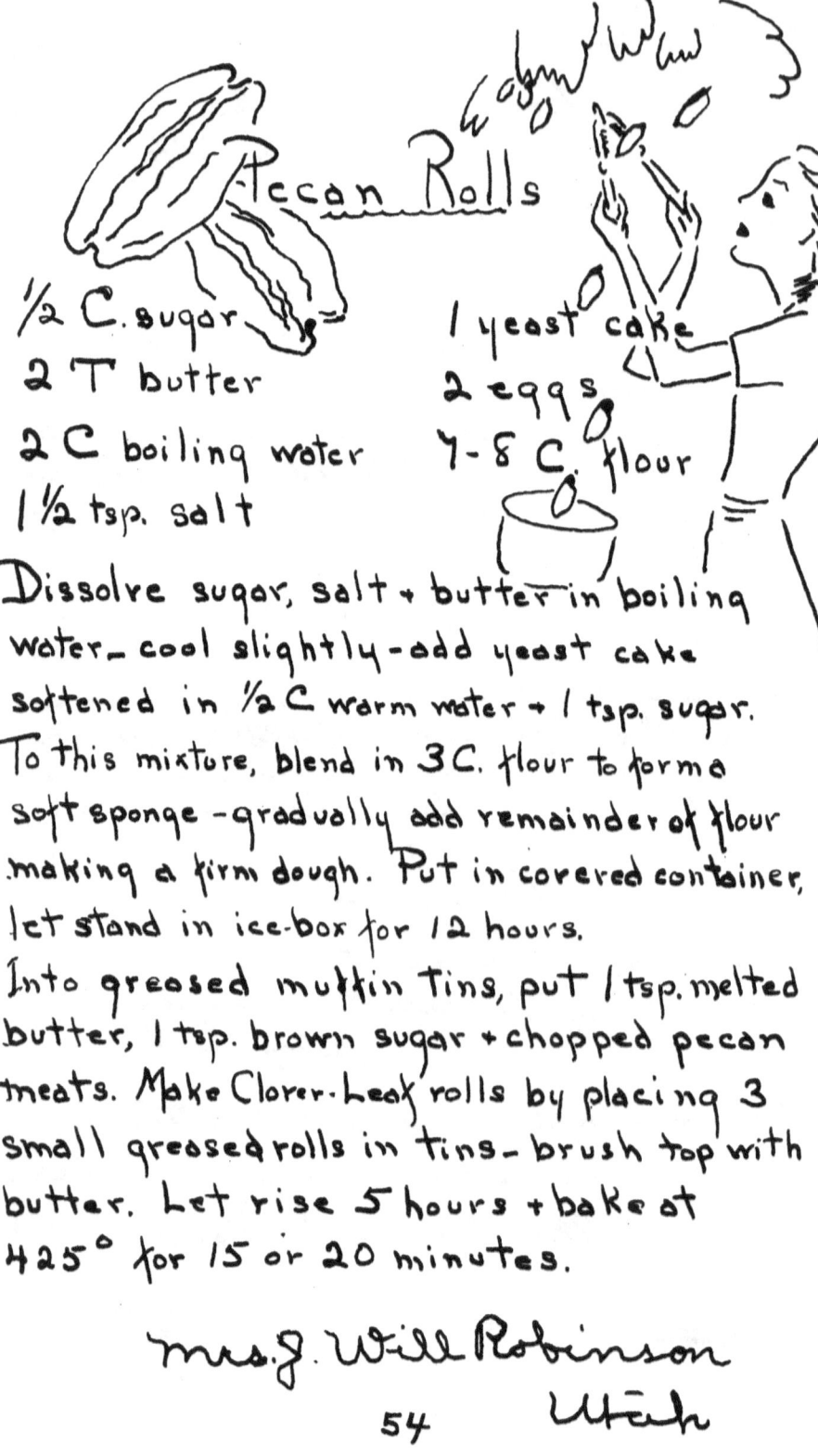

½ C. sugar
2 T butter
2 C boiling water
1½ tsp. salt
1 yeast cake
2 eggs
7-8 C. flour

Dissolve sugar, salt + butter in boiling water – cool slightly – add yeast cake softened in ½ C warm water + 1 tsp. sugar. To this mixture, blend in 3 C. flour to form a soft sponge – gradually add remainder of flour making a firm dough. Put in covered container, let stand in ice-box for 12 hours.

Into greased muffin tins, put 1 tsp. melted butter, 1 tsp. brown sugar + chopped pecan meats. Make Clover-Leaf rolls by placing 3 small greased rolls in tins – brush top with butter. Let rise 5 hours + bake at 425° for 15 or 20 minutes.

Mrs. J. Will Robinson
Utah

Refrigerator Rolls

Combine 2 c. boiling water
           2 T. butter
           2 T. sugar and cool until lukewarm.

At the beginning soften 2 cakes compressed yeast in ¼ c. lukewarm water. Later add 1 tsp. sugar. Combine the two mixtures and add 1 beaten egg. Then add 7 c. sifted flour and stir well. Put into refrigerator for at least 6 hours. Shape rolls and let rise until double in bulk (2-2½ hours). Bake in 425°F. oven for 12 minutes.

                     Mrs. H. Carl Andersen
                     Minnesota

Refrigerator Rolls
(Makes 3 doz. clover leaf rolls)

1 cake Compressed Yeast
1/2 cup sugar
1 teaspoon salt
2 cups lukewarm milk
1 egg
7 cups enriched flour, sifted
2 Tablespoons melted shortening

Crumble yeast into large mixing bowl. Add sugar, salt, and milk. Add well beaten egg. Add half flour, and beat well. Then add melted shortening, and mix in remainder of flour. Let rise to double its bulk. Punch down, cover tightly with waxed paper, and place in the refrigerator. About 1 1/2 hours before baking, remove desired amount of dough. Shape into small rolls, and place on greased pan. Let rise slowly to double their bulk. Bake in hot oven, 425°F. for 20 to 25 minutes.

Mrs. Arthur Winstead
Mississippi

Rolls

1 small potato boiled.
1 3/4 cups water
2 Tablespoons sugar add to potato with 1 Teaspoon salt.
3/4 cake of yeast.

Work 1 tablespoon lard in 3/4 Sifter of flour, add above. Start rolls at 9 or 10 — at 3 make into rolls bake 15 or 20 minutes in hot oven

Mrs. Edward Emmett Lowe
Kansas

Sally Luan Muffins

1 Cake of yeast
1 cup milk - scalded and cooled
1 Tbsp. Sugar
2 Tbsp. melted butter
2 Cups sifted flour
1 egg
1 tsp. Salt

Dissolve yeast and sugar in lukewarm milk. Add butter, then flour, egg well beaten and the salt. Beat until perfectly smooth. Drop into well greased muffin rings and let rise one hour in warm place. Cook in oven one hundred degrees.

Mrs. Herbert C. Bonner - North Carolina

Scotch Scones

1 qt. flour.
2 rounded tsps. B.P.
2 even Ts. sugar.
2 even Ts. butter.
2 eggs. Pinch of salt.
#
Add milk until mixed to a soft dough – Cut in small triangles. Bake in moderate oven for 15 min.

Mrs. George W. Gillie.
Indiana

Southern Spoon Bread

3 C milk
1 C white corn meal
1 tsp melted butter
1 tsp sugar
1 tsp salt
3 beaten egg yolks
3 stiff beaten egg whites

Scald milk in double boiler, add corn meal, gradually, & cook 5 minutes stirring to make very smooth. Cool slightly and add butter, sugar and salt. Add egg yolks, then fold in egg whites. Bake in greased baking dish in a moderate oven, 350°, about 45 minutes. Serve hot from the dish in which it was baked, with plenty of butter.

  Mrs J. P. Buchanan
    Texas.

Spoon Bread

1 C. corn meal
2 C. sour milk
2 eggs
1 tsp. soda
½ tsp. salt
1 tsp. shortening

Beat eggs, add milk, soda + salt. Sift in meal and lastly melted shortening. Pour batter in well greased casserole. Bake 20 minutes in moderate oven or until pudding is set then cut in center with knife.

Mrs John M Robsion
Kentucky
61

Swedish Biscuits

1 Pint Milk
1 Cake Yeast
2 T. Butter
1 Cup Sugar
2 or 3 Eggs, well beaten

Scald and cool milk. Dissolve yeast in a little water and sugar; Mix ingredients; Add enough flour to make a sponge; Let rise until light; Add more flour to make a dough to bread; Let rise and make into biscuits.

Mrs. Martin F. Smith
(Washington)

Waffles

2 C. heavy cream
2 C. flour
1 T. cornmeal
2 eggs
1 tsp. soda
½ tsp. salt

Sift flour, measure; sift all dry ingredients together twice. Beat egg yolks well and combine with sour cream. To this add dry ingredients gradually. Beat egg whites stiff and fold in last. If medium weight cream is used add 2 T. (scant) melted butter for crisper waffle.

Mrs. Edward T. Yarbrough
West Virginia

Waffles

2 c flour
2 t baking powder
3 T sugar
2 eggs, separated
1 1/4 c milk
6 T melted shortening

Sift flour and measure. Add baking powder, salt and sugar and sift again. Beat egg whites until stiff but not dry, then set aside. Beat egg yolks, add milk. Add dry ingredients and mix enough to blend. Add melted shortening. Preheat electric waffle iron, pour on batter. Bake for 4 to 5 minutes.

— Mrs. Malcolm C. Turner Georgia

Western Gold Waffles

1 pt. milk
1 pt. flour
3 eggs
½ cup melted butter (or shortening)
2 tsp. baking powder (medium)
add salt if shortening is used.

Beat egg yolks well
Beat melted butter into yolks
Add dry ingredients and milk alternately
Beat all thoroughly
Fold in beaten egg whites

This can be mixed ahead of time for later use if baking powder and egg whites are kept out and added when ready to use.

          Mrs Harris Ellsworth
            Oregon

West Virginia Spoon Bread

2 C. of meal
2½ C. of boiling water
3 T. of melted butter
1½ tsp. of salt
2 eggs
2 C. of buttermilk
1 tsp. of soda

Add cornmeal gradually to boiling water. Let stand until cool. Add butter, salt, egg yolks slightly beaten, buttermilk with soda. Beat well, and add whites of egg, beaten until stiff. Turn into buttered baking dish. Bake in hot oven 40 minutes.

Mrs. Chapman Revercomb
West Virginia

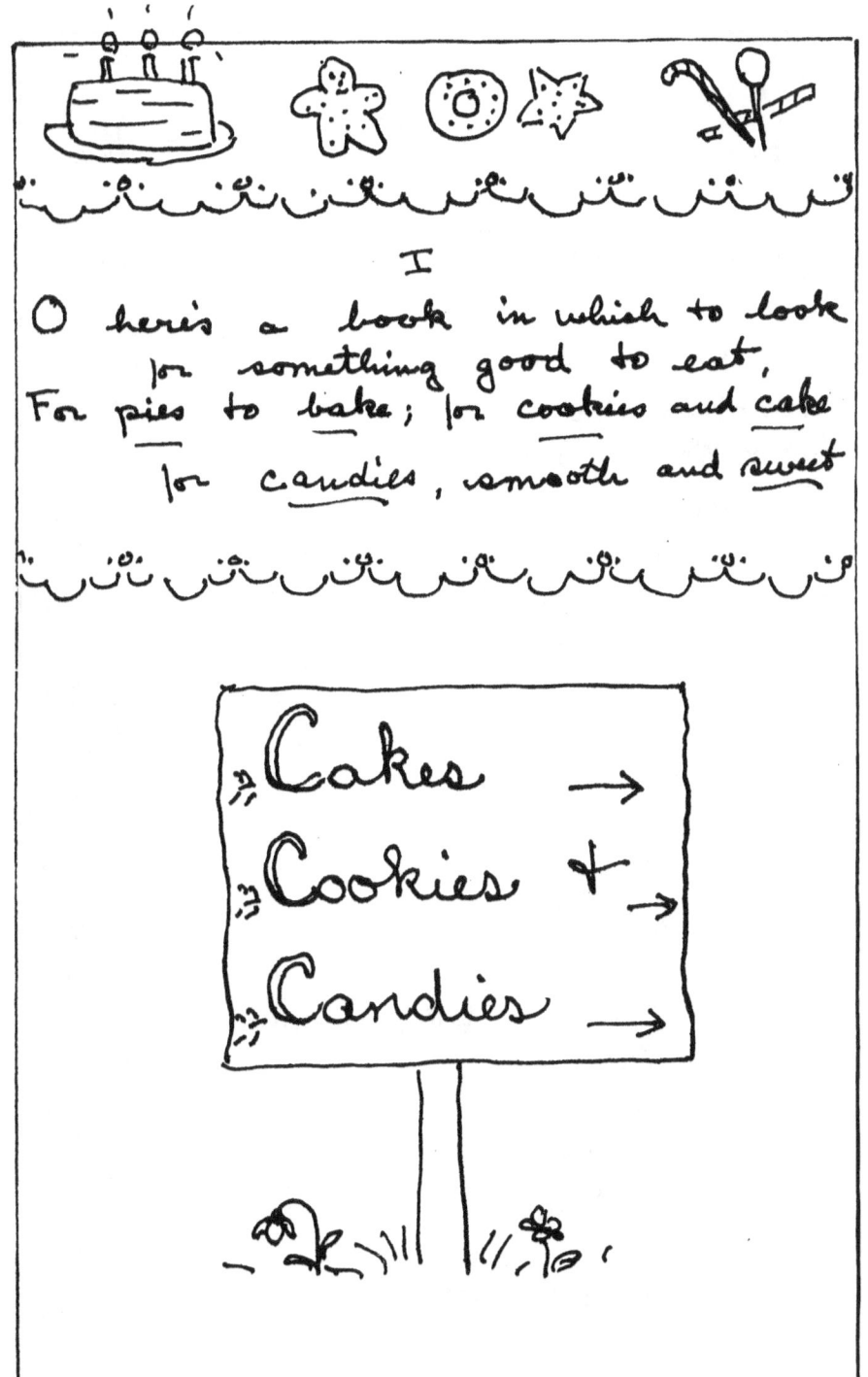

I

O here's a book in which to look
for something good to eat,
For pies to bake; for cookies and cake
for candies, smooth and sweet

Cakes, Cookies, and Candies Index

Banana Cake	70
Biscochitos (Spanish Cookies)	71
Bishops Cake	72
Black Walnut Yumyums	73
Brownies	74, 75
California Nut and Raisin Cake	76
Chinese Chews	77
Chocolate Cake	78
Cocoanut Cake	79
Cup Cakes	80, 81
Date and Nut Cake	82
Doughnuts	83, 84
Dream Bars	85
Fig Cookies	86
French Chocolate Cake	87
Frosted Chocolate Drop Cookies	88
Frosted Creams	89
Fudge Squares	90
Ginger Snaps	91
Gumdrop Cookies	92
Hermits	93
Honey-Oatmeal Cookies	94
Jam Cake	95
Lace Cookies	96

Marie's Orange Cookies	97
Mince-meat Upside Down Cake	98
Molasses Cake with Raisin Filling	99
Nut Cookies - Jam Centers	100
Oatmeal Ice-box Cookies	101
Pecan Cookies	102, 103
Pecan Dreams	104
Pecan Drops	105
Orange Slice Cookies	106
Raisin Crown Cake (Babka)	107
Small Date Cup Cakes	108
Sour Cream Cookies	109
Southern Jam Cake	110, 111
Sunshine Cake	112
Two Minute Cake	113
Van den Bergers (Doughnuts)	114
White Layer Cake	115
White Mountain Cake	116

Candies

Cream Candy	117
Peach Leather	118

"Butter and honey shall he eat." Isa. 7-15

Banana Cake

1 1/2 C sugar
1/3 - 2/4 C butter
1 tsp soda (scant)
1 tsp vanilla
1 C nut meats

2 eggs
2 C flour
1/4 c sour milk
1 C mashed Bananas

Cream butter & sugar, add beaten eggs, mix with milk (in which soda has been dissolved) stir in Bananas, nuts & bake. Serve with whipped cream.

Mrs C. W. Bishop, Wife of Congressman Bishop (Illinois)

Biscochitos (Spanish Cookies)

Cream   1 C. sugar
           ½ tsp salt
           ½ C lard. <u>no other</u> <u>shortening</u>

add   3 whole eggs one at a time.
           ½ tsp anis suds.

add   about 3 C flour more may be added to roll dough out to ¼ in thickness. Cut into any shape and dip top side into a mixture of granulated sugar and cinnamon. Bake in moderate oven 15 mi.

           Mrs. A. M Fernández
           New Mexico

Bishops Cake

3 eggs } Combine and beat
1 Cup sugar } well

1½ Cups sifted all-purpose flour
1½ tsp. baking powder
¼ tsp. salt
¼ lb. semi-sweet chocolate chips
2 Cups chopped walnuts
1 Cup coarsely cut dates
1 Cup halved candied cherries

Bake in a loaf pan in a 325° oven.

Serve as any fruit cake — does not need "aging" before using.

        Mrs. Dudley R. White
            "   " Ohio

Black Walnut Yumyums

½ C. butter
1 C. granulated sugar
2 well beaten egg yolks
1 tsp. vanilla
1½ C. cake flour
1 tsp. baking powder
Few grains salt
2 egg whites - beaten until stiff
1 C. light brown sugar or coffee sugar.
1 C. chopped black walnuts.

Cream butter, add sugar gradually. Cream well. Add egg yolks and vanilla. Sift flour twice and measure with baking powder. Spread cake mixture about ⅓ inch deep. in greased pan. In egg whites, fold in brown sugar. Add walnut meats and spread over cake mixture. Bake 30 minutes in moderate oven. When cool cut in squares or strips.

Mrs. Clarence J. Brown
Ohio

Brownies

¼ lb butter (melted)
1 C sugar
2 eggs (unbeaten)
½ C cocoa
½ C sifted flour
½ C nut meats
1 tsp vanilla

Break nuts into small pieces; mix well in the order given; pre-heat oven at 350°F for 15 minutes; bake in a greased pan 20 minutes; cut into squares while hot and dust with powdered sugar when cool.

Mrs. Clarence Cannon
Missouri

Brownies

6 level T. of cocoa
3/4 C. butter
2 eggs
1 C. sugar
1 C. finely chopped nuts

1 C. sifted flour
1 tsp. baking powder
1 Tsp salt
1/2 tsp. vanilla

sift together

Combine melted butter and cocoa. Mix well. Beat eggs slightly. Add sugar and flour mixture. Stir in cocoa and butter mixture. Add vanilla + chopped nuts. Pour into a warm greased shallow pan lined with greased paper. Spread the mixture evenly. Bake at 300° to 325°F for 45 min. to 1 hour. Turn from the pan and remove the paper while the cake is hot. Slice in thin strips.

Mary Barbara Cole
Missouri

California Nut and Raisin Cake

1 C. seeded raisins
1 C. sugar
½ C. shortening
2 eggs
½ tsp. each cinnamon, cloves, nutmeg, allspice

1½ C. flour
½ tsp. salt
¾ C. raisin liquid
1 C. walnuts
1 tsp. soda
1 tsp. vanilla

Simmer raisins 20 min. in 1½ cup water; cool; mix sugar and shortening; add eggs, well beaten; spices and vanilla, beat; add flour, salt, and liquor from raisins, add chopped raisins and nuts: beat thoroughly add soda, dissolved in a little hot water.

Filling:- Beat 1 egg, add ⅛ lb. melted butter, 2C. powered sugar; ¾ tsp. vanilla.

Mrs. Albert E. Carter
California.

Chinese Chews

1 c. dates, cut
1 c. pecans, cut
1 c. sugar
¾ c. flour
2 eggs
1 tsp. baking powder in flour
¼ tsp. salt

Beat eggs & add to sugar. Sift flour over dates & nuts. Add sugar & eggs to flour & nuts. Spread mixture on buttered pans and bake 40 minutes at 325°-350°- Makes 20.

Mrs. Walter E. Brehm
Ohio

CHOCOLATE CAKE
(NEVER FAILS OR FALLS.)

½ CUP BUTTER
1 CUP GRANULATED SUGAR
  CREAM TOGETHER
ADD YOLKS OF 2 EGGS
2½ SQUARES OF BITTER CHOCOLATE MELTED OR 5 TABLESPOONS OF COCOA
1 TEASPOON OF VANILLA
  PINCH OF SALT
MIX TOGETHER THOROUGHLY THEN ADD:
½ CUP MILK ALTERNATIVELY WITH 1½ CUPS OF FLOUR TO WHICH 2 TEASPOONS OF BAKING POWDER HAS BEEN ADDED. LASTLY FOLD IN THE WELL BEATEN WHITES OF 2 EGGS. BAKE IN A GREASED AND FLOURED SQUARE CAKE PAN ABOUT HALF AN HOUR AT 325°. USE FUDGE ICING.

  FROM AN OLD RECIPE.
  MRS. CLAUDE R. WICKARD.
      INDIANA

Cocoanut Cake

3 eggs
1½ C. sugar
1½ C. flour
1½ tsp. baking powder
Pinch of salt
} Sifted together 3 times.

¾ tsp. vanilla
1½ tsp. butter - melted
¾ C. milk - heated

Beat the eggs, add sugar + flour mixture then vanilla and butter. Heat milk and add. Bake in a sheet pan at 350° for 20 to 25 minutes.

Frosting

Melt 6 T. butter, add 10 T. brown sugar, 4 tsp. cream, 1 C. grated cocoanut. Mix well. Spread on warm cake and broil for 3 minutes.

Mrs. Wm. H. Link
Illinois

Cup Cakes

1 C butter   ½ tsp salt
2 C sugar   1 tsp vanilla
3 C flour   3 tsp baking powder
4 eggs   1 cup milk

Cream shortning + sugar thoroughly, add vanilla + eggs beat until fluffy. Add sifted dry ingreedients alternately with milk mixing thoroughly after each addition. Bake in 3 greased 9 inch layor cake pans 350°, 25-30 minutes. This recipe may also be used for Silver or Gold Cake. For Silver cake use 5 egg whites in place of 4 egg. For Gold cake use 5 egg yolks in place of 4 eggs.

Mrs J. P. Buchanan
Texas

Cup Cakes

Break one egg in a cup; add enough butter to make the cup half full, then fill with sweet milk.

Have in a bowl
1½ C flour
1 C sugar
2 tsp baking powder

add the cup mixture and beat vigorously until the batter is smooth. Add a small pinch of salt and flavor to taste. Put in muffin tins and bake for about 20 minutes at 375°F.

    Mrs. Clarence Cannon
        Missouri

Date Nut Cake

4 eggs — beaten separate
1 C. sugar
1 C. sifted flour
1 tsp. Baking Powder
1 tsp salt
2 seven ounce packages seeded dates — chopped.
1 lb. broken pecan Meats
1 tsp. vanilla

— Beat egg yolks thoroughly, add sugar. In separate bowl sift flour, salt & baking powder. Add chopped dates & Nuts. Combine two mixtures. Fold in beaten egg whites. Add vanilla. Bake in deep cake pan in slow oven for one hour.

Mrs. Robert L. F. Sikes
Florida

Doughnuts

2 cakes Fleischman's yeast plus
    1 tsp. sugar
1/4 cup warm water
2 cup scalded milk
1 tablespoon butter
1 tablespoon Crisco
2 eggs
2/3 cup sugar
1 tsp. salt
5 cups sifted flour (about)

Soften yeast plus 1 teaspoon sugar in warm water. Add shortening to scalded milk. When lukewarm, add eggs, sugar, salt and part of flour mix well. Add yeast and the rest of the flour. Butter should not be too stiff. Let rise overnight. In the morning toss on floured board and knead for 1 minute. Place batter in greased pan, put in a warm place. Cover and let rise for ½ hr. Toss again on floured board, cut in squares or rectangles, 2 inches by 3 inches and ½ inch thick. Place cut pieces on floured cloth, cover and let rise 2½ to 3 hours. Fry in deep fat until brown. Use a small high pan frying 3 doughnuts at a time. Serve hot, rolled in powdered sugar.

    Mrs. George H. Bender
      Ohio

Dream Bars

First mixture:
1/2 cup melted butter
1/2 cup brown sugar
1 cup flour

Mix and press into 10x15 inch pan. Bake 10 minutes in slow oven. Cool.

Second mixture:
1 cup brown sugar
2 tb. flour
1 1/2 cups cocoanut
2 eggs
1 ts baking powder
1 cup nuts
1 ts vanilla

Beat sugar, eggs and vanilla until smooth. Add sifted flour and baking powder and blend well. Then add cocoanut and nuts. Spread over baked crust and bake 20 minutes in moderate oven. Cool. Cut in bars.

Mrs. Max Schwabe
Missouri

Fig Cookies

1 C sugar 2 tsp. baking powder
½ C crisco 1 tsp. soda
1 egg 1 tsp. vanilla
  pinch of salt
½ C sweet milk
4 level cups of flour

Filling
½ lb. chopped figs
¾ C water
1 C sugar

Cream crisco and sugar add egg, milk, vanilla and dry ingredients. Roll thin and cut cookies. Put a tsp. of fig filling on each cookie. Place another cookie on top and press edges with fork. Bake at 450 degrees until brown.

Mrs Clinton P. Anderson
New Mexico

French Chocolate Cake

I.
- 1 c white sugar
- ½ c fat
- ½ c milk
- 2 c flour (scant)
- 2 tsp baking powder
- 2 eggs – salt – vanilla

II.   In double cooker:
- 3 squares chocolate
- ½ c milk
- ¼ c white sugar
- 1 egg yolk

Cook this until it thickens, let cool and add to part I.

Bake 25 min. in moderate oven.

Mrs A. Landy. Engel
Michigan

Frosted Chocolate Drop Cookies

Cream { 1 C. light brown sugar
       { 1/2 C. softened shortening

Add 1 egg - well beaten
    2 sq. melted chocolate

Mix 1/2 tsp. soda & 1 level tsp.
    baking powder with 1 1/2 C. sifted flour
Add alternating with 1/2 C. milk.
Stir in 1/2 C. raisins & 1/2 C. nuts.
Add pinch salt & 1 tsp. vanilla
Drop from tsp. on greased
pan. Oven 350. Watch. Bake
7-9 minutes.

Frosting.

2 C. XXXX sugar.
2 T cocoa   2 T melted butter.
Add enough strong black coffee
to blend. Spread on cookies.

Mrs. Charles F. McLaughlin
Nebraska

Frosted Creams

1 c. shortening
3/4 c. sorghum - part syrup if desired.
1 c. sugar
3 eggs (whole)
3 cups flour
1/2 tsp. ginger - more if desired
1 tsp soda
3/4 cup cool water

Mix in the order given beating well before you add the water. Bake in a shallow pan like jelly roll at 350°. Frost with powdered sugar frosting & cut in squares. Makes 30.

    Mrs Chas. B. Holven
        Iowa.

Fudge Squares.

Melt together over hot water.
½ cup cocoa
½ cup butter

Beat together
2 eggs
1 cup sugar,
and add

½ cup flour, 1 teaspoon baking powder, (sifted together) add 1 teaspoon vanilla, ¾ cup nuts, and butter mixture. Bake 20 minutes, moderate oven.

Mrs. J. Harry McGregor, Ohio

Ginger Snaps

1 C sugar
3/4 C shortening
1 egg (unbeaten)
4 tsp. dark molasses
2 C. flour
2 tsp. soda
1 tsp. ginger
1 tsp. cinnamon
1 tsp. cloves

Form into balls about one inch in diameter. Dip tops in a little sugar and place on ungreased cookie sheet about two inches apart. Bake at 275° about 18 minutes.

Mrs. August H. Andresen
Minnesota

Gumdrop Cookies

I. Mix and beat together
   - 4 eggs
   - 2 c brown sugar
   - 1 T. water
   - 1 tsp salt
   - ½ tsp baking powder
   - add 1 c flour to above

II. Mix 1 c flour.
    2 c spiced gumdrops & nuts.
Combine with egg mixture. Bake in two pans — moderate oven, about 25 min.

Icing

Combine
   - 3 T butter
   - 1 tsp grated orange peal
   - 2 T orange juice
   - 3 tsp brandy flavoring
   - XXX sugar to make good spread

cut in squares

Mrs Cleveland A Newton Missouri

Hermits —

½ cup shortening (generous)
1 cup brown Sugar

2 eggs
2½ cups flour sifted three times
1 scant cup buttermilk, in which
dissolve 1 scant teas. of Soda.
½ cup nuts chopped
½ lb. raisins
1 large Teaspoon allspice
1 "   "   cinnamon
½ teaspoon cloves

   Drop on cooky sheet and
bake about twenty five minutes
at 350-375.
   Makes 30-35.

              Bess W. Truman

Honey - Oatmeal Cookies

Spry — 3/4 cup
Strained honey — 1½ cups
Whole eggs — 2
Cinnamon — 1 teaspoon
Nutmeg — 1 teaspoon
Salt — ½ teaspoon

Flour — 1⅛ cups
Clabber Girl baking powder — 1 heaping teaspoon
Milk — ⅓ cup
Seedless raisins — 1 cup
Vanilla — 1 teaspoon

Quick oats — 3 cups

Blend spry and honey. Beat in eggs. Sift dry ingredients. Add to first mixture, alternating with milk. Add vanilla. Stir in raisins and oats. Nut meats — ½ cup — make a tasty addition. Drop by teaspoon on greased cookie sheets. Bake 15 minutes at 375° F.

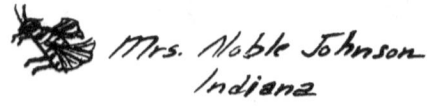

Mrs. Noble Johnson
Indiana

Jam Cake

1 cup of butter or shortening
1 ½ cups of gran. sugar
4 eggs
⅔ cup buttermilk
1 heaping tsp of soda
1 pint blackberry jam
1 tbsp. each of cloves cinnemon and allspice
Flour for medium batter.

Cream sugar and butter add the 4 free eggs. Disolve soda in buttermilk and add. Then the jam, spices and flour in order. Ice with either white or caramel icing.

Olga May Latta
Kentucky.

Lace Cookies

Mix

½ C. white sugar
½ C. brown sugar
1 C. Quaker oats - raw
1 tsp. baking powder
½ tsp. salt — 1 tsp. flavoring
½ C. melted butter
1 egg well beaten

Let stand until firm.
Drop by teaspoon 2 or 3 inches apart on greased + floured cookie sheet. Bake at about 300° for 4 or 5 minutes, until brown. Remove from oven — let stand until cookies harden.

Mrs. E. M. Dirksen
Illinois

Marie's Orange Cookies

1 cup shortening
3 eggs
2 cups sugar
Juice and Rind of 1 orange
4½ cups Flour
2 teaspoons Baking Powder
1 teaspoon soda
1 Tablespoon hot water
1 cup milk
1 cup nut meats
½ Teaspoon salt

Cream shortening – add sugar and eggs – Orange juice and rind – soda dissolved in hot water.
Mix – flour – salt – baking powder and add alternately with the milk add chopped nuts and drop by teaspoon on cookie sheet.

Frosting
1 pound package of powdered sugar – the juice and Rind of one Orange – dash of salt.

Mrs. Jerry Voorhis   California

Mince-meat Upside Down Cake

Mince-meat lining
- 1 table-spoon butter
- 1/3 cup sugar, white or brown
- 1 cup mince-meat

Cake-batter
- 1/3 cup butter
- 3/4 cup sugar
- 2 eggs
- 1/2 cup milk
- 1 1/2 cups pastry flour
- 1/4 tea-spoon salt
- 2 tea-spoons baking-powder

Butter the pan, sprinkle with sugar and line with mince-meat. Turn cake-batter over mince-meat and bake in moderate oven. Turn out while hot, serve with whipped cream or lemon-sauce.

Mrs. J. V. Heidinger.
- Illinois -

Molasses Cake with raisin filling

½ c. brown sugar
½ c. shortening
1 egg plus a second yolk
½ c. cold water
½ c. molasses
1 tsp soda
1 ⅔ c. flour
pinch salt

Method.
Cream shortening and sugar. Beat egg, plus yolk into mixture. Add molasses and cold water. Mix soda in a little hot water, just enough to dissolve. Add flour plus salt. Bake in slow oven about one half hour.

Raisin filling
1 c. sugar, ¼ c. water. Boil together until it threads. Add to stiffly beaten egg white, and ground raisins

Michigan   Mrs. Frank E. Hook

Nut Cookies - Jam Centers

½ C. Brown Sugar
½ C Butter
1 C flour
1 egg
½ C chopped nuts. Jam

Cream sugar and butter add slightly beaten yolk, then add flour. Roll into small balls, dip in slightly beaten egg white roll in chopped nuts and place on cookie sheet. Punch center with finger to make hole for jam. Bake in 350° oven for 5 min., take out and repunch holes, cook 15 min. more. Remove from oven and fill with jam while still hot.

    Mrs. Chet Halifield
      California

Oatmeal Ice-box Cookies

1 C Shortening	1½ C Flour
1 C Brown Sugar	1 tsp. Soda
1 C White Sugar	1 tsp. Salt
2 Eggs	3 C Quick Oats
1 tsp Vanilla	½ C Nuts

Cream shortening + sugar. Add beaten eggs + vanilla. Beat well. Add flour sifted with salt + soda. Add rolled oats + nuts. Shape into long rolls; chill; slice + bake at 350°.

Mrs James Dolliver

Iowa

Pecan Cookies

½ lb butter
2 C Sifted flour
6 T Powdered Sugar
1 scant tsp Salt
1 tsp Vanilla
1 tsp almond extract
1 C ground pecans

Cream butter and sugar, add other ingredients. Mix and chill in ice box. Roll in small balls, mash with bottom of glass. Bake at 325° until light brown.
Cool and dip in powdered sugar.

Mrs Karl Le Compte,
Iowa.

Pecan Cookies

3/4 C. shortening
1 1/2 C. brown sugar
1 Egg
1/2 tsp. salt
1/8 tsp. soda
2 C flour
1/4 C. chopped nuts
1/2 C whole pecans

Cream shortening, add sugar, add whole egg and mix. Sift salt, soda and flour together, add chopped nuts. Cover and let stand overnight in refrigerator. Form balls 1/2 in. in diam. Bake 8 to 10 minuits –

Mrs Ross Rizley
Oklahoma

Pecan Dreams

Part I

Cream ½ C. butter
      ¼ c xxxx sugar

Work in 1 c. sifted cake flour
        ¼ t. salt

Spread evenly in 8x9 pan.

Part II

Beat   2 eggs
Beat in   1½ C. Brown sugar
Beat in   2 T flour (all purpose)
          ½ t salt
          ½ t baking powder
          ½ t vanilla

Stir in   1 c pecans (chopped)

Spread over top of part I
Bake 35 min at 325°
Makes 30 squares

Mrs Edward R. Burke
Nebraska

Pecan Drops

Beat
   1 egg white – stiff
Stir in
   1 c. brown sugar
   ½ tsp. salt
   1 c pecan halves
Pick out with fork and spoon each pecan meat and dough that adheres. Place on buttered tin. Bake for ½ hour at 275° or until thoroughly dry. If some dough is left continue to add pecan meats.

   Mrs. E. M. Aitken
      Illinois.

Orange Slice Cookies

4 eggs, beaten
2 C. brown sugar
1 T. cold water
2 C. flour
1 Tsp. cinnamon
1 tsp. baking powder
pinch salt
} sift together

1 pound of orange candy slices, cut up with shears and floured, and
1 C. nuts meats

Take a square cake pan or one long one and flour lightly. Mix together above ingredients and pour into pan.

Glazing
Just before removing from the oven mix and spread on the following:

1 C powdered sugar
1 T. melted butter
3 T. orange juice

Put back in oven for two minutes. Cut in squares or fingers while hot.

Margaret Ayres Wergester
Kansas.

Raisin Crown Cake (Babka)

1 C. milk
2 cakes yeast
1 tsp sugar
½ C. flour
½ lb. shortening
¾ C. sugar
6 eggs
1 C. raisins
⅓ C. citron
⅓ C. chopped cherries
3 C. flour
1 tsp salt
½ tsp nutmeg
Almonds blanched
Bread crumbs

Scald milk. Cool, add crumbled yeast, sugar half C. flour. Set aside to rise. When light, add creamed shortening, sugar and beaten eggs; beat well. Add raisins, citron, candied cherries. Flour these before putting in. Sift measure flour, add salt, nutmeg and sift again. Add to first ingredients. Grease large tube pan, press blanched almonds around sides and bottom. Sprinkle with fine bread crumbs, pour in dough and let rise for one hour. Bake in preheated oven (350°) one hour or until baked. When cool invert on a plate, sprinkle with confectioners sugar.

Mrs. Thomas S. Gordon
Illinois

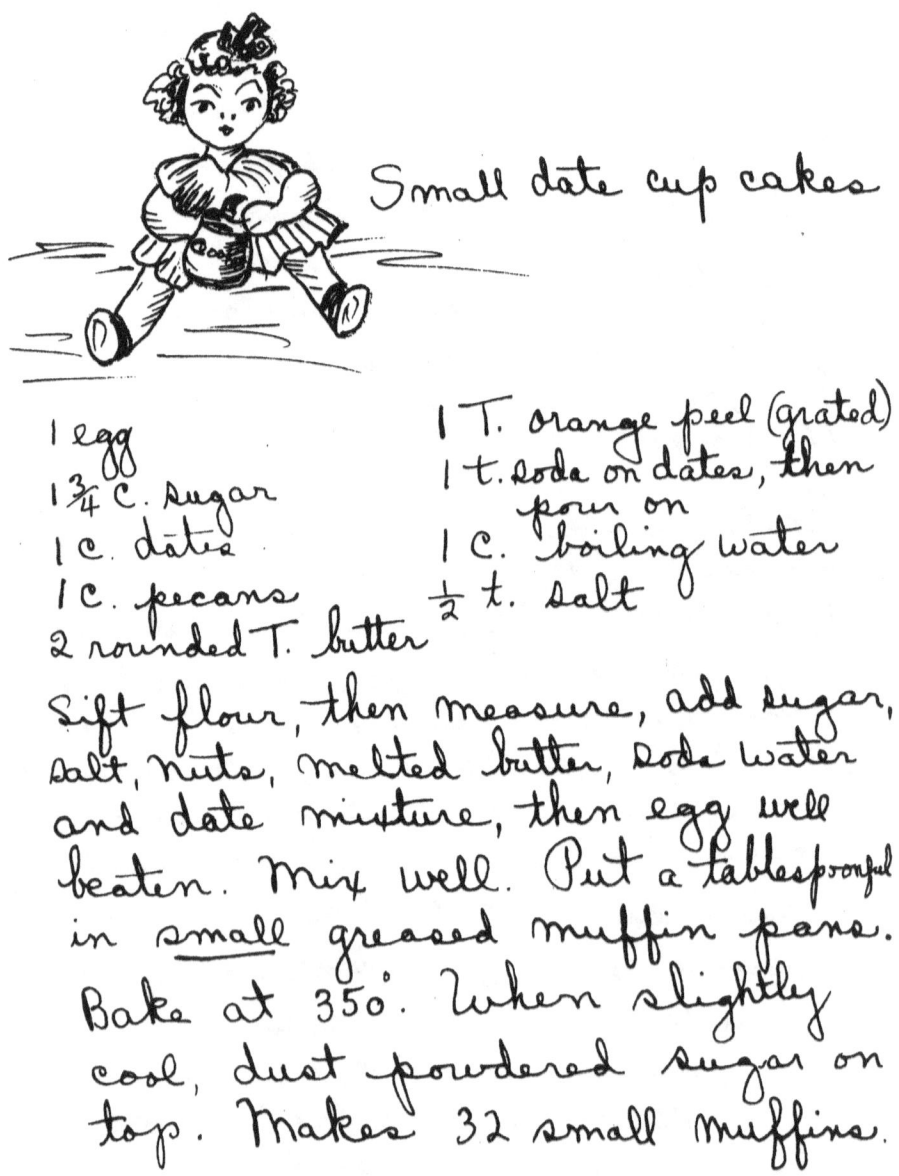

Small date cup cakes

1 egg
1 ¾ C. sugar
1 C. dates
1 C. pecans
2 rounded T. butter
1 T. orange peel (grated)
1 t. soda on dates, then pour on
1 C. boiling water
½ t. salt

Sift flour, then measure, add sugar, salt, nuts, melted butter, soda water and date mixture, then egg well beaten. Mix well. Put a tablespoonful in <u>small</u> greased muffin pans. Bake at 350°. When slightly cool, dust powdered sugar on top. Makes 32 small muffins.

Mrs. John Sparkman
Alabama

SOUR CREAM COOKIES

1 Cup butter.   1/2 tsp salt.
2 Cups sugar.   1 tsp vanilla.
2 eggs.   1 tsp baking powder.
1 Cup sour cream. 1 tsp soda (level)
4 Cups sifted flour.

Cream butter and sugar. Add eggs well beaten and one teaspoon soda in one tablespoon hot water. Mix one rounded teaspoon baking powder with four cups sifted flour. Add to dough with one cup sour cream. Bake 12 to 15 minutes. 400°.

Mrs. John M. Baer
NORTH DAKOTA

Southern Jam Cake with Orange Icing

3 eggs
2 cups sugar
1 cup butter
1 cup buttermilk
1 teaspoon soda
3 cups flour
1 cup jam (blackberry or rasberry previously strained)
1 cup raisins
1 cup nuts
1 teaspoon nutmeg
1 teaspoon spice
1 teaspoon cloves
1 teaspoon cinnamon

Dissolve soda in milk and mix with other ingredients. Bake in layers

Icing
3 oranges

1 grated orange rind
2 cups sugar
Butter ball the size of an egg
2 eggs (whites)
2 eggs (yolks)

    Beat whites and yolks of eggs separately. Then mix with other ingredients. Cook in double boiler over slow heat until thick enough to cover cake smoothly. Let cool before spreading between layers and on top of jam cake.
    Miss Annie Louise Rankin
        Mississippi

Sunshine Cake

- 7 egg yokes
- 1/4 c. Sugar
- 3 Tsp. warm water
- 1 tsp. salt
- 1 tsp. lemon extract
- 1/2 tsp. orange extract
- 1 tsp. vanilla extract
- 1 tsp cream of tarter
- 1 c. Flour
- 7 egg whites

1. Separate egg whites into large bowl and yokes into a smaller bowl. 2. Sift and measure flour and sugar. 3. Beat egg yokes until light yellow, to them add 3/4 c. of sugar and the warm water. Beat until fluffy. 4. Beat whites, adding, adding salt and cream of tartar, then beat until stiff. Add remaining sugar and beat well. 5. Combine egg yokes with the whites. Add flavoring Fold in flour. 6. Turn into an angel food pan well buttered and bake. Place into cold oven; Set temperature at 325°. Bake one to one hour and forty-five minutes. Ice if desired.

Mrs. Erland H. Hedrick
West Virginia

Two Minute Cake

2 C. flour
4 tsp. baking powder
1 tsp. salt
1½ C. sugar

Sift, mix together

½ C. Spry
1 C. milk
1 tsp. Vanilla

Beat 2 minutes in electric mixer. Add 2 whole eggs, beat 2 more mins. Bake in sheet tin, 325° oven, about 30 minutes.

Chocolate Fudge Icing

4 sqs. Chocolate
1 C. sugar
2 T. boiling water
2 eggs
⅓ C. butter

Mrs. Thomas J. O'Brien
Illinois

Vandenbergers

Beat 3 eggs
Beat in 2 C. sugar
Beat in 2 C. warm mashed potatoes
and 3 T. melted butter
Into ¾ C sour, stir ½ tsp soda, add to the
above, also add 1 tsp. salt, 4 tsp baking
powder + ½ tsp. mace or nutmeg.
Sift 5 C. flour. Mix in 4 cups. + add rest
as needed. Do not get the dough too stiff-
Roll out a part as needed.
This makes about 48 regular sized doughnuts
If you use a fancy cutter in shape of
◇ ♡ ♧ ♤ it will make 100
For frying use part Crisco + part Wesson
Oil. It is best to use an iron kettle. To
test the heat of the lard, drop in a tiny piece,
if it comes <u>immediately</u> to the top, the temperature
is right. It is very important to keep the
frying at an even temperature, so that necessitate
turning the heat up + down.

Mrs. Arthur Vandenberg
Michigan.

White Layer Cake.

1 T. Butter
1 c. granulated sugar
2 eggs (2 yolks – 1 white)
1 c. of milk
2 Level cups of flour (cake
2 Heaping tsp. Baking Powder
1 tsp. Vanilla

Bake – 375 – 20 min.

If you use sour milk – add ½ tsp. soda.

"Frosting"

1 cup maple syrup
boil slowly until it hairs.
Beat egg white with a fork on platter till fluffy, and it stands up.
Remove maple syrup from fire, and beat into egg white until creamy enough to spread.
Top with crushed walnut meats

Mrs. Bernard W. Kearney,
New York.

White Mountain Cake.

I Cream { 3 C. sugar
           1 C. butter.
Add 1 C. milk.
Beat whites of 6 Eggs very light.
Add ½ of egg whites to first mixture.

II mix { 1 T. baking powder
         4 C. sifted flour,
Add to first mixture little at a time.
Add 1 tsp. flavoring – stir, fold in
remaining egg whites bake in
moderate oven.

"Lemon cheese filling"

Yolks of 4 Eggs | juice of 2 lemons
2 C. sugar | 1 T. grated rind
1 T. butter | 1 C. boiling water
2 T. flour.

Mix all ingredients except flour, make
smooth paste of flour & little water, then
add to first mixture, stir well. cook
till thick, when cool spread between
layers. plain white icing may be
used for top & sides of cake.

Mrs Edward O McCowen
Ohio.

Cream Candy

3 C Sugar
3 C Water
3 T butter

Coloring, mint or desired flavoring

Pour water over sugar; stir until dissolved; boil but do not stir, until a little is dropped in cold water and forms a ball. Pour on a buttered marble slab; pour flavoring and coloring on candy, let cool until it can be taken up and pulled. Pull until white; return to marble, cut in small pieces with scissors. Place in candy jar or cake box to cream.

Mrs. Malcolm C. Tarver
Georgia

Peach Leather

A very old-time Eastern Shore Confection.

Peel and stone good ripe peaches. Cook in own juice until soft enough to mash through colander. While hot add to each pint of puree ½ cup granulated sugar. Spread thinly and evenly on bottom of clean, dry tray or cookie pan. Place in hot sun, cover with screen. Let dry until not sticky. Sprinkle lightly and evenly with granulated sugar. Roll as firmly as possible. Wrap in wax paper. Store in tight, dry container. Cut in ½ inch lengths when used.

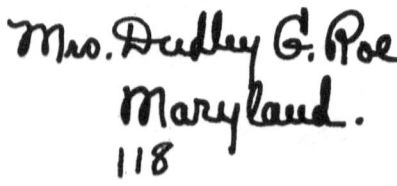

Mrs. Dudley G. Poe
Maryland.

Desserts Index

A Delicious Dessert	122
Apple Crunch	123
Apple Quickies	124
Apricot Souffle	125
Brownie Pudding	126
Charlotte Russe	127
Cherry Charlotte	128
Chocolate Cream Souffle	129
Chocolate Mousse	130
Chocolate Torte	131
Cocoanut Dessert	132
Crême Brulée	133
Date Puddings	134, 135
Date Crumb Pudding	136
Indian Pudding	137
Lemon Pudding	138
Lemon Souffle	139
Lemon Sponge	140
Persimmon Pudding	141
Plum Pudding	142
Raisin Pudding	143
Suet Pudding	144

Texas Pudding	145
Butterscotch Sauce	146
Honey Sauce	147 ← Sauces
Maple Syrup Dressing	148
Frozen Apple Sally	149
Frozen Apple Sauce	150
Frozen Pineapple Cream	151
Graham Cracker Ice Cream	152
Lemon Ice Cream	153 Frozen
Lemon Cream Sherbet	Type 154
Lemon Sherbet	155
Pineapple Ice Cream	156
Pineapple Sherbet	157
Refrigerator Ice Cream	158

"She brought forth butter in a lordly dish." — Judges V-25

oooooo (6 points please)

A Delicious Dessert

1 Pkg. Phila. Cream Cheese
2 Tbsp. Honey
¼ Pt. Sour Cream

Mix and chill for 24 hours. Serve with crushed fruit. This is very delicious with crushed strawberries.
Don't fail to try this sometime.

Mrs. Jed Johnson.
Oklahoma

Apple Crunch

6 apples   1 cup sugar
1/4 cup cream   1/4 ts nutmeg
   juice of one lemon

Peel and slice apples, place in baking dish. Cover with sugar, nutmeg, cream and lemon juice.

Top mixture:
1 cup flour   6 tb crisco
1 egg   2/3 cup sugar
   salt

Cream crisco and sugar, add egg and salt and beat until light and fluffy. Add sifted flour and blend well. Spread this mixture over apples and bake in moderate oven (350°) 50 to 60 minutes.

Serve with cream

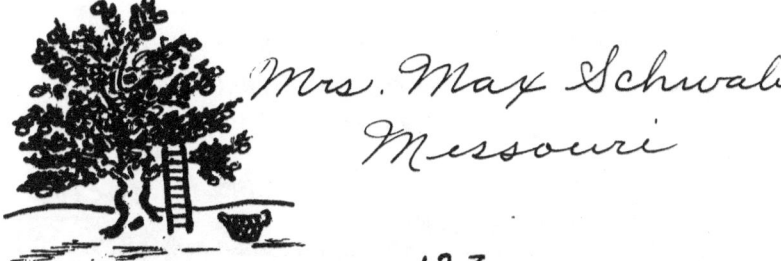

Mrs. Max Schwabe
Missouri

Apple Quickies

Maraschino Apple Sauce

Save the liquid from bottles of maraschino cherries as they are used and cook ordinary apple sauce in it. The apple sauce will have a delicate flavor and color.

Apple Cocktail or Salad

To a commercial can of fruit salad add one or two apples cut up into ½ inch cubes. Serve either as a fruit cocktail or as a fruit salad with proper embellishments.

Baked Halves of Apples

Select large firm tart red apples. Cut in halves. Remove cores. Fill hollows with a few raisins and a little flour mixed into about 1 T. of sugar per half apple. Put a dab of butter on top of filled hollow. Place in baking pan, pour in boiling water to cover bottom of pan, and bake until tender, basting often, at 400°.

"Comfort me with apples." - S. of S. 2-5

Mrs. Hal Holmes
Washington

Apricot Souffle

1 No. 3 can of Apricots,
1/3 cup of sugar,
3 egg whites,
1/2 teaspoon almond flavoring.

Drain juice from apricots, rub them thru a sieve or food mill, add sugar to pulp and simmer 10 min. Cool. Fold in beaten egg whites, add flavoring. Bake in greased individual molds in a pan of hot water, 1/2 hour at 350° degrees.

Serve with sauce made of the juice and two tbsps of brown sugar and one of corn starch and small lump of butter.

Serves six.

Mrs. Wm. S. Hill,
Colorado

Brownie Pudding

1 C. flour
2 t. baking powder
½ t. salt
¾ C. gran. sugar
2 T. cocoa
½ C. milk
1 t. vanilla
2 T. melted shortening
1 C. chopped nuts
¾ C. brown sugar
¼ C. cocoa
1 ¾ C. hot water

Sift flour, baking powder, salt, gran. sugar, and cocoa. Add milk, vanilla, and shortening, mix until smooth. Add nut meats. Pour into well greased square cake pan. Mix brown sugar and cocoa; sprinkle over batter. Bake at 350°, 40 or 45 minutes.

Mrs. George Grant
Alabama

126

Charlotte Russe

1/2 pint cream
3 eggs
1/2 cup sugar
1 envelope gelatine.

Beat cream stiff, add whites beaten stiff. Beat yolks with sugar. Moisten gelatine with little cold water, then add 1/4 cup hot water to dissolve gelatine and strain onto yolks and sugar. Mix thoroughly and add to cream & whites. Flavor with vanilla, set on ice beating till it forms — Line mold with lady fingers & fill center with cream

Mrs. Daniel L. Reed New York

127

Cherry Charlotte

1 qt. sour cherries
1 C. sugar
¼ C. water
Pinch of salt
Buttered white toast.

Stone and cook cherries with water + sugar until tender. In a qt. bowl, put alternate layers of toast + cherries. Place weight and plate on contents + put in ice box 6 or 7 hours. (Juice will all be absorbed). Unmold on serving plate + cover completely with whipped cream.

    Mrs. Joe Hendricks
    Florida

Chocolate Cream Soufflé

Combine in top of double boiler: 1/3 cup minute tapioca, 1/2 cup sugar, 1/4 teaspoon salt, 2 squares unsweetened chocolate, cut in pieces, 2 cups milk. Place over rapidly boiling water and cook 8 to 10 minutes, after water boils again, stirring frequently. Add 2 tablespoons butter. Cool slightly. Beat 3 egg yolks until thick. Beat 3 egg whites until stiff. Add egg yolks to mixture and blend. Fold into egg whites. Turn into greased baking dish. Place in pan of hot water. Bake in moderate oven (350° F.) until soufflé is firm. Serve hot with cream.

Mrs. J. P. Buchanan, Jr.,
Texas.

Chocolate Mousse

2 sq. unsweetened chocolate, or 2/3 c. cocoa
1 c. cold milk
1 T gelatin, soaked 5 min. in 1/4 c cold milk
1/2 c. Sugar (if made with cocoa 1/3 c.)
1/8 tsp. salt
1 c. cream
(Top of milk is preferred if allowed to stand 48 hrs.)
1/2 tsp. vanilla

    Heat chocolate and milk in double boiler until chocolate is melted. Beat with hand egg beater 1 min. while still heating.
    Add soaked gelatin, sugar, salt. Stir until smooth. Cool.
    Place bowl on ice, add cream and vanilla. Chill until cold and syrupy.
    Whip from 10 to 20 min. until consistency of whipped cream.
    Pour into freezing tray of refrigerator with regulator set at coldest temperature. Leave for 3 hrs.

Mary Park Clements
Georgia

Choclate Torte

8 eggs - 8 yolks - 4 whites
4 whites for meringue
2 c. sugar
½ c chopped blanched almonds
4 bars sweet chorlate
1 c. crackers rolled fine
2 T. allspice - 2 t cinnamon
1 T. cloves - rind and juice of lemon
Mix above ingredients together
and bake in slow oven 1 hour.
Put glass of tart jelly on
torte while still hot - top with
the meringue and put back
in oven to brown.

Mrs. Charles La Follette
Indiana

Cocoanut Dessert

1 c. milk
1 c. sugar
1 pt. heavy cream
1 heaping T gelatine soaked in ¼ c. cold water.
salt + vanilla
2 c. fresh cocoanut

Heat milk + add sugar + soaked gelatine. Cool. When it starts to thicken beat with a Dover beater then add cocoanut, whipped cream and vanilla. Put in a ring mold + let stand in ice box over night and serve with

Caramel Sauce

1½ C brown sugar
½ c Karo syrup
2 tab. butter.

Boil to soft ball and thin with cream when cool.

Mrs. Dow Harter
Ohio

Crême Brulée

7 yolks of eggs
1 pt. whipping cream
½ cup brown sugar
Pinch of salt.

Heat cream in double boiler for 25 min. Beat yolks of eggs slightly, add pinch of salt then add cream. Return to double boiler, cook until soft custard, strain into shallow pyrex dish, cool and sprinkle brown sugar over top, then run dish under hot flame – let sugar melt which will form crust on top. Put in ice-box and serve cold

Mrs. Richard B. Wigglesworth
Massachusetts

Date Pudding

6 eggs
2 cups sugar
1 pkg. chopped dates
10 rounded tablespoons
   of cracker crumbs
1 cup nuts

Cream together sugar and egg yolks. Add to this mixture chopped dates which have been mixed with cracker crumbs and nuts. Fold in beaten egg whites. Bake in slow oven 45 minutes. Serve topped with whipped cream or ice cream.

Olga May Latta
Kentucky.

Date Pudding

32 soft dates seeded and cut up with knife.
½ C. granulated sugar
1 C. English walnuts broken with fingers

Mix these and add:

1 heaping T. flour
1 teasp. baking powder
4 T. sweet milk
1 egg well beaten

Stir these in and pour into well buttered baking dish. Bake 50 minutes in very slow oven. Serve with cream.

Mrs. John Phillip
California.

Date Crumb Pudding

2 eggs
½ C sugar
3 T milk
2 T melted butter
1 tsp vanilla

1 C dry bread crumbs
1 tsp. baking powder
¼ tsp salt
1 C chopped dates
½ C chopped nuts

Beat eggs in mixing bowl, gradually beat in sugar. Add milk, melted butter & vanilla & mix well. Add bread crumbs mixed with baking powder + salt, then stir in dates & nuts. Pour into well greased 9 inch pie pan, or small baking dish. Bake about 40 minutes in slow oven 325°F. Serve warm or cold with chilled custard sauce, or whipped cream. Makes 6 servings.

Mrs. Frank Carlson
Kansas

Indian Pudding.

4 C scalded milk
in double boiler
add 5 T corn meal
cook 20 min.
mix 2/3 C molasses
    1 tsp. ginger
    ½ tsp. salt
    2 T butter
add to corn meal mixture
put in baking dish
pour scant ½ C milk
over pudding
bake in slow oven
3 or 4 hours

    Mrs Leverett Saltonstall
      Massachusetts
(my husband's favorite dessert)

Lemon Pudding

1 cup sugar
4 table spoons flour
1/8 teaspoon salt
Stir together and add
2 tablespoons melted butter
5 tablespoons lemon juice and grated rind of one lemon.
3 egg yalks beaten
1 1/2 cups milk
3 egg whites beaten
Bake in custard cups in moderate oven.

    Mrs. Daniel L. Reed
       New York

Lemon Souffle

1 lemon
1 C. sugar
4 eggs – separated

To the sugar add the grated rind and juice of lemon. Mix.

Beat egg yolks until thick and lemon colored. Add to above mixture. Blend well.

Beat egg whites until stiff. Fold into mixture gently.

Put in baking dish, set in pan of hot water and bake forty minutes at 325°. Serves four.

Mrs. P.W. Griffiths
Ohio

Lemon Sponge

3 eggs - rind of 1 lemon and juice
1 C Sugar
2 T flour
1 C milk

Add sugar, lemon rind and flour to beaten egg yolks. Add lemon juice and milk slowly - Fold in beaten egg whites. Cook in pan of water, as in baked custard - About 325° degrees until brown

Mrs. Herbert C. Bonner
North Carolina

Persimmon Pudding

1 quart persimmons
1 quart milk
1 tsp. baking powder
2 c. flour
1 egg
1 tsp. soda
1 tsp. vanilla
1½ c. sugar

Wash persimmons (the small ones, not the large cultivated kind) and put through a colander; add other ingredients; put in buttered pan and bake very slowly for three hours, stirring frequently while baking except the last one half hour.

Margaret Ayres Weigester
Kansas.

Plum Pudding

6 eggs
1½ C soft bread crumbs
1 tsp. salt
1 C flour
1 C sugar
2 tsp mixed ground spices
   1 C currants
   2 C seeded raisins
   ⅔ C mixed candied fruit
   2 C chopped beef suet
grated rind of 2 lemons
1 C grape juice or brandy

Mix currants, raisins and peel. Add suet lemon rind sugar, spices sifted flour salt and bread crumbs. Moisten with beaten egg and grape juice. Turn into well greased molds or bowls and steam 6 hr. Replace water as it boils low.

      Mrs. Hugh Peterson, Georgia.

Raisin Pudding

1 cup flour
2/3 cup sugar
1/4 tsp. salt
1½ tsp. baking powder
add.
1 C seedless raisins
½ C milk
Put in a greased pan 8-10
Boil
2 C water
1 C B. sugar firmly packed
2 T butter
Pour over mixture & bake
350° - 30 min.
Serve with whipped cream.
Good without.

   Mrs Wilson D. Gillette
    Penna

Suet Pudding

1 Cup chopped suet
1 Cup buttermilk
1 Cup molasses
1/2 Cup brown sugar
3 eggs
3 cups flour
1 tsp soda
1 tsp cloves
1 tsp cinnamon
Steam 2 1/2 hours
Slice and steam as needed; serve with hard sauce

Mrs. Roy O. Woodruff
Michigan

Texas Pudding

4 egg yolks.
1-2 cup of sugar.
1-2 cup sherry wine.
1 pt. whipped cream.
4 egg whites.
1 cup pecan meats.
1 slice crystallized pineapple.
1 bottle maraschino cherries.

Cook in double boiler the egg yolks, sugar and wine until thick.
Set aside to cool.
Whip cream and egg whites seperately, then mix. Add to cooked mixture.
Add crystallized pineapple, cherries (without juice) and pecans. Freeze.

Mrs. Lindsay C. Warren.
North Carolina.

Butterscotch Sauce

1½ C. light brown sugar
4 T. margarine
⅔ C. white corn syrup

Stir constantly over low heat until mixture boils. Boil until it forms soft ball in water. Cool. Add ⅔ C. heavy cream or 1 small can evaporated milk.

Fudge Sauce

3 sqs. bitter chocolate
1 C. granulated sugar
1 tsp. Vanilla
1 C. evaporated milk
¼ C. water
½ C. white corn syrup

Melt chocolate over hot water. Add water slowly, stir until smooth. Add sugar + syrup. Boil to soft ball in cold water. Remove from fire. Add milk + vanilla + mix.

Both sauces will keep in icebox + remain soft when poured on ice cream.

Mrs. George Outland
California

Honey Sauce.

- 1 c powdered sugar
- 1/3 c butter
- 3 tbsp. cream
- 6 tbsp. strained Honey
- 1 tsp vanilla or rum

Cream sugar and butter add slowly cream then honey and flavoring. Use on Hot Fruit pies dumplings - mince meat pie - or warm for steamed puddings

Mrs. Harlan J. Buschfield

South Dakota

Maple Syrup Dressing

1 egg. 1 C maple syrup.
Juice of ½ lemon.

Beat egg slightly with a fork, add syrup, and lemon juice, stirring constantly. Chill. Add two table spoons or more, according to taste to one cup of whipped cream.

    Mrs. Porter H Dale
      Vermont.

Frozen Apple Sally

Use any good apple sauce recipe, with tart apples. Freeze in freezer, or in electric refrigerator, beating well when almost frozen. Serve with whipped cream and mixture of ¾ sugar and ¼ nutmeg.

    Mrs. Robert A. Taft
        Ohio.

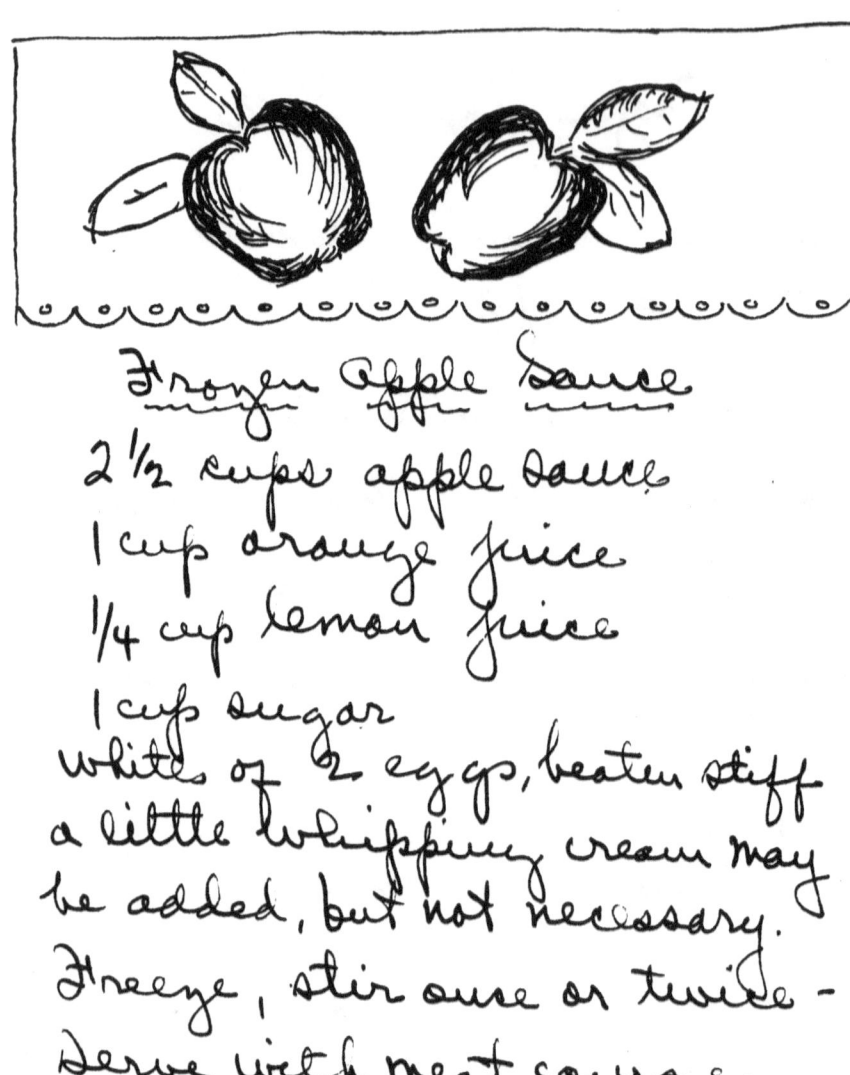

Frozen Apple Sauce

2½ cups apple sauce
1 cup orange juice
¼ cup lemon juice
1 cup sugar
Whites of 2 eggs, beaten stiff
a little whipping cream may be added, but not necessary.
Freeze, stir once or twice -
Serve with meat course

Mrs Orville Zimmerman
Missouri

Frozen Pineapple Cream.

1. can crushed pineapple.
1. packet marshmallows.
1 pint whipping cream.

Soak marshmallows which have been cut up with the crushed pineapple over night or for several hours. Whip cream and add to this mixture.
Pour into ice tray and freeze to firm consistency.

Mrs Estes Kefauver
Tennessee.

Graham Cracker Ice Cream

1 Scant C Graham Crackers
1 Scant ½ C sugar
1 Pint Coffee Cream
1 tsp Vanilla
 pinch salt

Mix all together and freeze. When frozen remove to chilled bowl, crush and beat until light and fluffy. Put back in tray and freeze.

Mrs Wm. Lemke
North Dakota.

Lemon Ice Cream

Beat two eggs
Add the following
   ½ c sugar
   ½ c light corn syrup
   1 t grated lemon rind
   ¼ c lemon juice
   2 c top milk
   (or 1 c milk + 1 c cream)
Mix well.
Pour into shallow refrigerator trays. When partly frozen, pour into chilled bowl and whip.
Freeze until firm.
Serves 4 – 6

         Vivian Bestal
           Indiana

Lemon Cream Sherbert

2 C. milk   Add
1 C. sugar

7 T. lemon juice
Grated rind 1 lemon
Add lemon juice & rind to first
mixture slowly, stirring well.

1 C. cream
2 egg whites
2 T. sugar
Beat egg whites, not stiff,
add sugar slowly.
Whip cream to thick custard.
Combine egg and cream
mixture: add to frozen
mixture that has been well
beaten. Return to refrigerator
to finish freezing.
Orange juice or any crushed
fruit may be substituted for
the lemon juice.

Mrs. George B. Schwabe
Oklahoma

"And she opened a bottle of milk."
— Judges IV-19.

Lemon Sherbet.

Whip one large can of cream (all brands will whip if chilled) add the juice of four lemons, in which one cup of sugar has been dissolved. Add the grated rind of one lemon, and one cup of rich top milk or thin cream. Freeze with coldest control. It is not necessary to stir it, but several stirrings will keep the creamy, fluffy consistency. Serves eight.

Mrs. Eugene Cox, Georgia

Pineapple Ice Cream

1 c. crushed pineapple
1 pt. of top cream from milk
    or coffee cream
1 c. sugar
1½ c. water

    Boil water and sugar five minutes. Cool.

    Add pineapple and cream. Mix well.

    Put into a freezing tray in refrigerator and freeze fast. Stir once while freezing.

        Mrs. Earl Wilson
            Indiana

Pineapple Sherbet

2 cups Buttermilk
3/4 " sugar
1 " crushed pineapple
1 egg white

Freeze until half frozen. Add a little of the sugar to egg white and whip. Add pineapple mixture and whip until light and fluffy adding 1/2 teaspoon Vanilla. Pour in tray and finish freezing.

Mrs Wright Batman Texas.

Refrigerator Ice Cream

1 pt. coffee cream
1 c. cookie crumbs
   (use crisp cookies)
¼ c. sugar
1 tsp. vanilla

Roll cookie crumbs very fine
Add to cream
Add sugar and vanilla
Beat all ingredients until well dissolved
Pour into tray and freeze
When mixture becomes stiff remove from tray and beat well
Refreeze

Note — If graham crackers are used, this is delicious with a fresh fruit sauce.
If chocolate cookies are used, this may be served with a chocolate sauce.

Mrs. Jamie L. Whitten
Mississippi

— Favorite Dishes Served at the Club by Miss Young —

— (For You From Us) —

Index of Miss Young's Dishes.

Baked Prune Whip	161
Bran Muffins	162
Carrot Ring	163
"Essie's" Chicken	164
French Dressing	165
Gingerbread	166
Lima Beans - Creole	167
Meringues	168
Shepherd Pie	169
White Cake	170

Baked Prune Whip

4 lbs. prunes soaked overnite.
Cook in small amount of water until tender
Remove seeds + put thru grinder
Mix with
6 c. sugar
¼ tsp salt
Add to
28 egg whites beaten stiff.
Butter 2 medium flat pans + put in
mixture - Bake at 300° about 1 hr.
Serve with custard sauce, made with
15 egg yolks - slightly beaten
3 qts milk
⅛ tsp salt + 1 T. Almond extract.
Cook in double boiler + cool.
= Serve 50 =

Bran Muffins

¾ c. shortening
½ c. brown sugar
2 c. molasses   } mix together
5 eggs
4 c. milk

Add 5 c. All Bran + let stand about 20 mins. until bran softens.

Add
5 c. flour
4 T. baking powder } sifted twice
1 T. salt

Drop in greased muffin tins + Bake 30 mins. at 350°
= 50 large muffins =

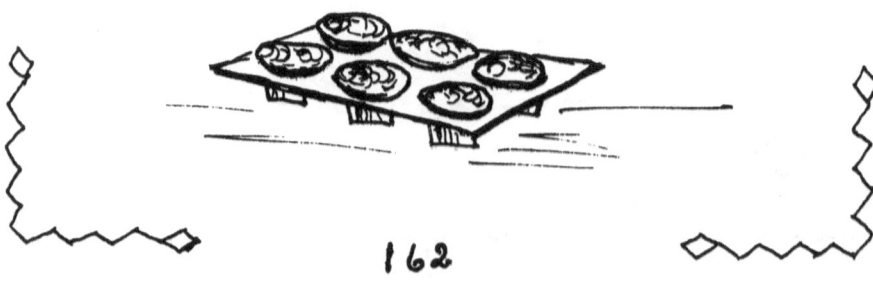

Carrot Ring

2 T. butter or margarine
4 T. flour
¾ c milk
4 eggs - separated
2 c. hot mashed carrots
1 c. soft bread crumbs
1 tsp salt

Melt butter in top double boiler - Add flour + blend. Add milk + slightly beaten egg yolks. Cook until thickened.
Add carrots - crumbs + salt, blending well.
Remove top from boiler + fold in stiffly beaten egg whites.
Turn into well greased 10" ring mold.
Bake at 350° for 30 mins -
Turn out + fill ring with cooked peas
= Serves 8 to 10 =

Essie's Chicken

Quarter 2 to 3 lb. fryer
Salt + pepper
Sear in deep fat (very hot) for 3 mins.
Dip in flour, then in an egg wash
Roll in bread crumbs

Place in roaster, the bottom of which is covered with water - about ½ c.
Brush chicken with butter or substitute.
Cover + put in oven, steam until tender
About 1 hr. at 300° - Add water if needed.

French Dressing
(½ gal.)

- 3 T. salt
- 3 T. sugar
- 3 T. dry mustard
- 3 T. paprika
- 1 c. strained honey

} mix together

- 1½ qts salad oil
- 1 pt cider vinegar
- 2 cloves of garlic

Put in jar with tight top & shake vigorously —

— Shake each time used —

Gingerbread

2 C. shortening } cream
2 C. brown sugar } together

Add 6 eggs
   4 C. molasses
   4 C. hot water

10 C. flour
 6 tsp. soda
 4 tsp. cinnamon   } sift together
 4 tsp. ginger   } &
 1 "   clove   } Add to Above
 1 "   allspice
 2 .   salt

Bake in 2 pans, 10"x14" at 350°
for 40 mins.

Lima Bean - Creole

5 lbs. dried lima beans, soak overnite
Cook with ham trimings or hock - DRAIN.

5 large onions
5 green peppers } Chopped & Sauted
1 lb. or more bacon or ground ham

Add
1 #10 can tomatoes
3 T. salt
½ T. pepper

Mix + bake in flat pans at 350°
for one hour -
— Serve 50 —

Meringues

12 egg whites beaten stiff
3 c. sugar added gradually
1 T. vinegar
1 T. vanilla
¼ tsp. salt

Put in pastry tube + drop on brown paper in individual rings.

Bake very slow, 50 mins to 1 hr in oven less than 250°. The oven must never be hot.

This makes about 45

Fill with ice cream or fruit.

Shepherd Pie

5 lbs. shoulder veal ⎫ cut for stew
5 lbs   "   lamb ⎭ free of bone

Brown in skillet, in which 3 or 4 large onions have been sauted, Add 1 gal water or chicken stock, 3T. salt, 1 tsp. pepper. Let simmer until tender. Thicken liquid & add cooked sliced carrots & peas. Put in medium flat pans,

Boil & mash 5 lbs white potatoes, Add salt do <u>not</u> add milk, beat in 5 egg whites one at a time. Put this on top of meat mixture with a #31 Ice Cream scoop –

Place in oven at 400° until browned –

= Serve 50 =

White Cake

1½ c. shortening } cream together
3 c. sugar

Add 9 egg whites unbeaten, one at a time

½ tsp salt
5 c. sifted cake flour } sifted together 3 times
5 tsp baking powder

2 c. milk

Add flour + milk alternately to above mixture, beating slowly.

1 T. vanilla

Bake in sheet pan 13" x 19" at 350° for 30 mins.

   Frost when cool.

Fish and Fowl Index —

Asparagus Fillets	174
Baked Tuna	175
Crabmeat Noodle Casserole	176
Fish Turbit	177
Halibut Pudding	178
Holiday Oysters	179
Kedgeree	180
Lobster a la Newburg	181
Louisiana Gumbo A'la Creole	182
Minced Oysters	183
Noodle Surprise	184
Salmon Casserole	185
Salmon with Lemon Sauce	186
Salmon Loaf	187
Salmon Souffle	188
Scalloped Oysters	189
Shrimp Casserole	190
Shrimp on Holland Rusk	191
Tomato Sauce with Shrimp	192
Tuna Fish Supreme	193

Fowl

Barbecued Chicken	194
Buffet Chicken	195
Chicken and Noodles	196
Chicken Boo Yah	197

Chicken Mushroom Casserole	198
Chicken Pot Pie	199
Chicken with Wine	200
Escalloped Chicken Supreme	201, 202
French Stuffing (for Turkey or Chicken)	203
Freid Custard (with chicken)	204
Mock Chicken Legs	205
One Dish Meal - Chicken and Rice	206
Pheasant Casserole	207
Pressed Chicken	208
Scalloped Spaghetti and Chicken	209

Asparagus Fillets.

12 fillets of sole, cod or other white fish.
1. can asparagus tips or frozen asparagus could be used.
2. tablespoons butter.
2. tablespoons flour.
3. cups milk.
½ lb cheese or less.
½ teaspoon salt. pepper.

Wrap each fillet around several asparagus tips. Place with asparagus heads up in baking dish. Prepare cream sauce add half of amount of cheese. Pour over fish. Sprinkle remaining cheese over all. Bake in slow oven about 40 mins.

Mrs. Estes Kefauver. Tennessee.

Baked Tuna

Cover the bottom of a casserole ½ inch deep with Potato Chips.

Heat together
1 can Campbells Mushroom Soup
1 " Celery soup
1 - 7 oz. can Tuna Fish - (rinsed)

Pour over Potato Chips and cover top with chips
Bake ½ hr. at 350°.

Mrs Wilson Gillette.
Penna.

CRABMEAT-NOODLE CASSEROLE

2 T. Butter
1 C. Cream
2 pkg. Old English Cheese
   COMBINE
   Melt in Double Boiler

1 pkg Broad Noodles
   Cook
   in Salt Water
1 LB. Mushrooms
   Sauté
1 LB. Crabmeat
   Combine
Cook 1 Hr. - Moderate Oven

Mrs. Rolla C. McMillen
Illinois

Fish Turbit

3 T. flour
1 T. butter
1 C. boiling milk
1 can salmon steak
Seasonings
Bread crumbs

Make a white sauce with the flour, butter + milk. Add seasonings, the flaked fish + mix well. Place in individual ramekins + sprinkle with rolled bread crumbs + dot with butter.

Place ramekins in pan with shallow water, keeping water well below a boil + bake until cooked through.

Mrs. Earl C. Michener
Michigan

Halibut Pudding.

1 lb. halibut (or haddock) raw
1 pint cream
1 " bread crumbs.
   (stale, white, ground up)
onion juice to flavor
celery salt " "
Whites of four eggs

Grind halibut, add bread crumbs, seasoning, beat egg whites stiff and fold in. Bake in slow oven 30 minutes — set in pan of water. Serve at once with cream sauce thickened with egg yolks, or lobster and mushroom sauce — flavored with sherry.

          Mrs. Robert Hale
          State of Maine

Holiday Oysters

½ c milk
½ c chopped onion
2 c " celery
1 T " green pepper
3 T butter or substitute
3 c cooked wild rice - drained
½ t salt   ¼ t sage
⅛ t thyme   ⅛ t pepper
1 pint oysters
3 T butter or substitute
½ c bread crumbs

Brown onion, green pepper, and celery in fat. Blend in flour, add milk slowly (may need more milk). Stir in hot rice and seasonings. Place in shallow, greased pan. Dip oysters in melted butter and then in crumbs. Arrange in layer over cooked rice mixture. Sprinkle with crumbs and remaining melted butter. Place under broiler with low flame. Cook until oysters curl or about 15 minutes. Serve with mushroom sauce. Serves six.

Mrs. Dean P. Taylor
New York

KEDGEREE

1 c. any boiled white fish (flaked)
1 c. boiled rice
2 hard boiled eggs
Seasoning to taste

Mix all ingredients together. Heat again and serve hot. (The hard boiled eggs are, of course, chopped and added. If one likes the mixture a little moist, milk may be added.)

Can be served with a tomato sauce.

Frank Roosevelt

Lobster a La Newburg.

1 1/2 C. Lobster meat
1 T. butter
1/2 C. sherry wine
1 C. cream
Yolks ③ eggs

Cut lobster meat into small pieces and place in double boiler with butter, salt and pepper. Pour over this the wine and cook for 10 minutes. Add beaten egg yolks and the cream. Bring to a boil and serve in patty shells or on toast.

Mrs. Dwight L. Rogers,
Florida.

Louisiana Gumbo a la Creole

1 # ham
1 # okra (or 1 can)
2 doz. raw oysters
6 hard-shell crabs (or 1 # crab meat)
1/2 gal. oyster liquor, stock or water
4 onions
4 pods garlic
1 T flour
1 large can tomatoes
Dash of salt, pepper, thyme, parsley.

Fry diced ham, set aside. Fry sliced, fresh okra (brown) set aside. Brown flour, chopped onions, garlic, add tomatoes. Let simmer for 5 min. Stir in oyster liquor or water, add seasonings. Next add crabs, (previously scalded, cleaned, quartered) or crabmeat, peeled shrimp, ham, okra, simmering for 2 hrs.

Serve hot in soup plates with mounds of boiled rice, steamed dry. Serves 10 persons.

Mrs. Allen J. Ellender
Louisiana.

Minced Oysters

1 Quart Oysters
1 Tea Spoon Celery seed
½ Tea Spoon black pepper
1 Tea Spoon salt
⅛ Tea Spoon Red pepper
4 Eggs
¼ lb. butter or Margerine
1 cup Chopped Celery
1½ cups Cracker Crumbs

Mince the oysters with Scissors. Add Seasonings, and the whole Eggs. Put on Stove in a Sauce pan. Stir Constantly until it reaches the boiling point. Remove and add cracker Crumbs to thicken. Put in Baking dish. Slice Butter over the top and cut through mixture. Bake in a moderately hot oven (375°) until brown on top.

Mrs. John Jennings Jr
Tennessee

Noodle Surprise

1 Can tuna fish — 3½ oz.
1 Can mushrooms   4 oz.
  or fresh oven sauteed
3 cups medium thick cream
        sauce
1 Box flat noodles
¼ lb pimento cheese

Cook noodles in slightly salted boiling water. Drain and peel to pieces tuna fish, drain and cut mushrooms in half, slice cheese very thin. Mix all ingredients, pour into baking dish, bake in medium oven 20 minutes, and brown in top of oven.

Mrs. Ralph W. Gwinn
New York

Salmon Casserole

1½ C. cooked salted noodles.
1 can mushroom soup
1 C. milk
1 can salmon (or tuna)
½ C. cracker crumbs.
Salt and pepper.

Add milk to soup. (If tuna is used pour boiling water through it to remove oil.) Shred salmon.
Put into a casserole a layer of noodles, salmon then crumbs. Cover with soup mixture. Repeat.
Brown in oven 450°.

Mrs Earl Wilson
Indiana

Salmon with Lemon Sauce

1 tall can Red salmon
2 C sweet milk
2 T. flour
1 tsp. salt
Juice of 2 lemons
2 whole eggs
Red pepper + nutmeg to taste

Put milk on to boil. Make paste of flour + oil from can of salmon. Add to boiling milk + cook until thick. Take off stove + beat eggs through the sauce. Add juice of lemons, red pepper, nutmeg + last of all, the salt. Pour this sauce over the salmon which has been flaked in a large platter. This dish is good either hot or cold.

Mrs. W. J. Norrell
Arkansas

Salmon Loaf

1 can salmon
3/4 c. bread crumbs
2 T. flour or 1 T cornstarch
2 T butter
2/3 c. milk
1 egg
2 T. minced onion
3/4 tsp. salt
1/4 tsp. paprika

Method

Add 1/2 c. white sauce to bread crumbs, salmon, egg, and season.

Grease baking dish and bake in moderate oven 350° for 35 minutes.

Mrs. Frank E. Hook
Michigan

Salmon Soufflé

2 Tbls. butter
3 Tbls. flour
½ cup scalded milk
½ Teas. salt
Few grains cayenne
1 cup flaked salmon
3 eggs separated

Melt butter
Add flour
When well mixed
add gradually
scalded milk.
Add salmon, salt and cayenne
Remove from fire
Add well beaten egg yolks
Cool
Cut and fold in well beaten
egg whites.
Pour into buttered baking
dish and bake 20 to 25 minutes
in slow oven. Serve at once.

Mrs. John Taber   New York

Scalloped Oysters

1 pint Oysters
1/4 pound Butter
1 pint Cream

Butter medium Casserole, cover bottom with broken Crackers then place layer of Oysters, Repeat having Crackers as the top.
Salt and Pepper
Add the Cream and chunks of butter. Should be quite juicy.
Let stand in cold place for one hour.
Bake 30 minutes in 400° Oven or until heated thoroughly and is brown.

   Mrs Kenneth S Whevvy
    Nebraska

Shrimp Casserole

2 lbs shrimp
1 can tomatoes
3 slices bread
1 pepper
1 onion
3 tbsp chili sauce
3 hard boiled eggs
Salt and pepper

Chop pepper and onion, brown in butter. Soak bread in tomato. Add shrimp, then add mixture to pepper and onion. Let cook about twenty minutes. Add chili sauce and chopped eggs. Put in greased baking dish and cover with bread crumbs.

Mrs Fred Bradley,
Michigan

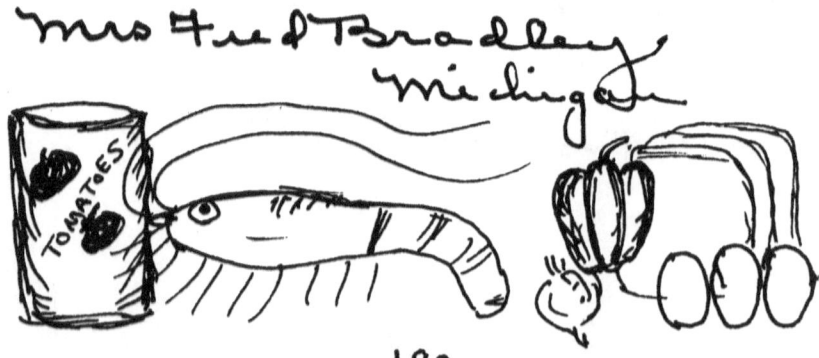

Shrimp on Holland Rusk

Spread each piece of rusk thickly with cream cheese seasoned to taste. Cover with slice of tomato, then shredded lettuce, and top with shrimp. Just before serving cover with sauce.

Sauce.
3/4 c. Wesson oil
1/4 c. vinegar
1/2 c. Chile sauce
1/4 c. water
1/2 c. sugar
1 tsp. each, salt and paprika
juice of medium-sized onion - mix thoroughly.

Mrs. H. M. Whittington
Mississippi

Tomato Sauce
With Shrimp over Eggs

1 tablespoon butter
1 cup boiled shrimps
1 can condensed tomato soup
3/4 cup milk or cream

Melt butter and saute the shrimps. Then add tomato soup with milk or cream and heat. A little chopped parsley and a bit of garlic added just before serving adds flavor. Pour over boiled eggs.

Mrs Clarence F. Lea
California

Tuna Fish Supreme.

1 can Tuna Fish
1 Small Bag Potato Chips
1 can Mushroom Soup.

Drain the tuna fish and pour boiling water over it. Break into small pieces. Save out a handful of potato chips and roll the rest of them fairly fine. In baking dish put alternate layers of the tuna fish and potato-chip crumbs, adding tiny pieces of green pepper. Pour the mushroom soup (diluted according to directions on can) over it, and put remaining potato chips on top, and sprinkle with paprika. Bake about 30 minutes in moderate oven.

Mrs. Augier L. Goodwin
Massachusetts.

Barbecued Chicken

Juice of four lemons (approximately)
1/4 medium size bottle Catsup
1/4 bottle Lea & Perrins sauce
1/2 lb. butter or margarine
Black & red pepper, salt & paprika to taste.

To Mix: Squeeze lemons in porcelain pan. Add catsup, sauce, butter and seasoning. Let ingredients come slowly to a boil. Cut four young chickens in halves. Broil under blaze having a slow heat. Turn often, basting constantly with sauce, using a pastry brush.

Mrs. Arthur Winstead
Mississippi

Buffet Chicken Mexican style

- 1 - 4 lb. chicken
- 2 T olive oil
- 1 c sliced celery
- 1 green pepper chopped
- 1 clove garlic chopped
- 1 onion chopped
- 4 c stewed tomatoes
- ½ t curry powder
- Salt & pepper to taste
- ½ c sliced blanched almonds
- 1 c cooked fresh mushrooms
- 1 c ripe olives
- 2 c whole kernel corn
- ½ c cheese grated
- 1 pkg noodles

Boil chicken until tender, cool, cut in small pieces. Save broth. Fry chopped onion, garlic, green pepper & celery in olive oil. Add tomatoes & curry powder. Add salt & pepper. Simmer 1 hr. Add almonds, chicken, corn, mushrooms & olives. Boil noodles until tender in chicken broth. Drain & save broth for soup. Add noodles to first mixture. Place in casserole. Sprinkle with cheese & heat slowly in oven 250 degrees for 1½ hrs.

Mrs. Dean P. Taylor
New York

Chicken and Noodles

One large hen, boil with celery, onion, salt & pepper. Save stock to cook 1 box noodles, 15 min

Chop a small can of ripe olives, pimento, drain off juice.

Sauté in butter & juice of half a lemon, ½ lb of fresh mushrooms, salt & pepper. Cutting chicken as you would for salad.

Make a thick cream sauce, season with salt, pepper & paprika. To this add enough cooking sherry to taste & thin. Mix all above ingredients, except noodles.

When ready to serve put noodles in bottom of baking dish, chicken mixture on top. Sprinkle generously with Parmesian cheese & bake in medium oven until cheese is golden brown.

Mrs Albert Thomas
Texas

Chicken Boo Yah

3-4 lb Chicken
1 C. each celery, carrots
   potatoes - peas
½ C. each onion and parsley

Dress, clean, cut chicken in pieces. Add salt - pepper - boiling water - cook until tender. Add vegetables - diced - simmer until ready to serve - the longer the better.

Serve in large soup bowls as the main dish.

Mrs. La Vern R. Hilweg
Wisconsin

Chicken Mushroom Casserole

1 boiled chicken
1/2 lb. mushrooms
1/2 lb spaghetti
3 T. butter or chicken broth
2 T. flour
2 C. chicken broth
1 C. heavy cream
2 T. sherry
Parmesan cheese

Cut meat from bones of chicken. Cook spaghetti. Add sautéed mushrooms. Make a white sauce. Add seasoning. Remove from fire. Add heavy cream heated and sherry. Mix all ingredients. Place in greased baking dish. Sprinkle top with parmesan cheese. Bake in moderate oven (375°) until light brown. Serves 8-10.

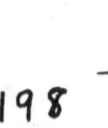

Mrs. George Grant
Alabama

Chicken Pot Pie

1 large chicken, cooked, seasoned + boned.
1 C or can of mushrooms.

Put chicken + mushrooms in large, deep casserole. Pour over White Sauce, top with Liquid Batter.
Bake in hot oven 35 minutes.

White Sauce
3 T. butter - melted
3 T. flour
1 C. top milk
3½ C. chicken broth

Liquid Batter
1 egg
1 C. flour
¼ tsp. salt
2 T. baking powder
½ C. butter - melted
1 C. warm milk

Mrs. M. E. Yeager
Ohio

Chicken with Wine

Have 2 chickens cut up. Brown lightly in butter or margarine.
Add 1 C. California white table wine. Cover. Simmer for 15 minutes. Add 1 pint of cream. Recover, simmer for another 15 minutes.
Add Seasonings.
Add small potatoes and mushrooms if desired. Cook until potatoes are tender. Add more wine if too much cooks away. Sauce may be thickened if necessary.

Mrs. Leroy Johnson
California

Escalloped Chicken Supreme

- 6 c. cooked chicken
- 6 c. cooked rice
- 4 c. chicken broth
- 3 c. milk
- 4 tbsp. butter
- ¾ c. flour
- 1 c. blanched almonds
- 1 small can pimento
- 2 c. mushrooms or 2 cans
- 1 tbsp. salt
- ⅛ tsp. pepper

Cook a 5 lb. chicken in water to cover with 1 tsp. salt, 3 stalks celery, 1 onion.

Pour 1 c broth over rice.

Make a rich gravy by adding the milk to 3 c. of the broth. Add butter blended with the flour. Season.

Arrange layers in this way:—

Rice, chicken cut in pieces, pimento, mushrooms fried lightly. Cover with buttered crumbs and almonds.

Bake at 350° for ¾ hr.

Mrs. Thomas E. Martin
Iowa

French stuffing for turkey or chicken
– 15 lb turkey –

- 2 lbs pork   } ground to-gether
- 1 lb round steak
- 5 medium potatoes – boiled
- 1 small onion
- Salt, pepper, parsley, clove, cinnamon to taste.

Cook meat with a little water until it's white, then mix all ingredients to-gether, add enough bread to take up extra liquid.

This may also be used for a pie with top crust, and may be eaten hot or cold.

Mrs Aime J. Forand
Rhode Island

Fried Custard
(Served with fried chicken)

SERVES 8

- 2 C. milk
- stick cinnamon
- 3 T. cornstarch
- 2 T. flour
- ½ C. sugar
- 1 tsp. butter
- ½ tsp. salt
- 4 egg yolks
- 1 tsp. vanilla
- 1 egg white
- 1 C. cracker crumbs

Put cinnamon in milk - boil 2 minutes. Take out cinnamon - make paste of Cornstarch and flour. Add to milk. Cook 3 min. - stir constantly. Add sugar, butter, salt & yolks. Cook 2 min. after putting in eggs. When cool, add vanilla. Pour into greased pan 6 by 10 in. Leave in ice box 12 hours or more. When ready to serve - cut custard into squares - dip into beaten egg whites - then cracker crumbs, and fry in hot butter in skillet. Drain on paper.

Mrs. Clifford Davis
Tennessee

Mock Chicken Legs

½ lb. veal } ground
½ lb. pork } together
1 tsp. minced onion
1 T. minced green pepper
1 T. minced celery
1 egg beaten, add ¼ C. milk
2 C. rolled corn flakes
Salt + pepper to taste

Set aside ½ of egg mixture + 1¼ C. corn flakes.

Mix all ingredients well, mold in pear-shaped rolls + put on to wooden skewers, dip each piece in egg mixture, then roll in corn flakes. Fry brown, place in covered dish or chicken fryer, add about ½ C. water + bake for 1 hour at 350°. Makes seven or eight chicken legs.

    Mrs. Chauncey Reed
        Illinois

One Dish Meal — Chicken & Rice

- 1 4 lb. chicken cut in sections
- 1 C. hot water
- 1 Tbsp shortening

- 2 quarts hot water
- 2 cans tomato soup
- 1 C. chopped celery
- 1 small onion
- 2 C. rice
- pepper, paprika
- 2 Tomato
- 1 green pepper, sliced
- 1 onion, sliced

Roll chicken in seasoned flour. Place in greased roaster. Pour on shortening melted in hot water. Bake 1½ hours at 350°. When brown remove sections and cover. To liquid in roaster add 2 quarts water, tomato soup, celery, onion and seasonings. Boil 5 minutes, scrape all brown from side of roaster into liquid.* Arrange each piece of chicken with slice of onion and tomato in green pepper rings. Bake until vegetables are done about 1 hour.

*add rice.

Mrs Karl Stefan.
Nebraska

Pheasant Casserole.

Skin the pheasant and draw as you would prepare a chicken. Cut in pieces for frying. After rinsing wipe each piece carefully, removing any stray feathers or shot. Roll in flour. Fry in generous amount of shortening to a golden brown. Place in covered roaster or casserole, season with salt and pepper, and add one pint cream.

Bake in moderate oven (375°) one hour. If liquid cooks dry during baking add a small quantity of milk or water. Serve with wild rice.

— Mrs. Karl Mundt
South Dakota.

Pressed Chicken

1 hen boiled until tender
3 hard boiled eggs
1 pint of chicken stock
2 T gelatin in 1-4 C cold water
Season highly with salt + pepper.

Remove meat from bone, grind in a food chopper or cut very fine. Boil the stock until reduced to a pint, add gelatin + thoroughly melt. Remove from fire + season. Line a bread pan with wax paper, put in a layer of chicken, through the center put the whole eggs, now the remaining chicken, over all pour the hot stock. Set aside to get firm. Unmold + slice.

Mrs. Stephen Pace
Georgia

Scalloped Spaghetti and Chicken

- 1/4 C. Chicken Fat or Shortening
- 1/4 c. Chopped Onion
- Salt and Pepper
- 1 C. Grated Cheese
- 1 C. Canned Tomatoes
- 2 C. Diced Chicken
- 1/4 C. Flour
- 2 c. Chicken Stock
- 1 8 oz. pkg. Cooked Spaghetti
- 1/2 C. Buttered Bread Crumbs.

Melt fat, cook onions slowly for 10 min. Add Flour, stir well, Add Stock, stirring constantly until Thickened. Add Salt and Pepper to taste. Add Cheese, stir until melted, Add Tomatoes and Chicken. Place Chicken mixture and Spaghetti alternately in a greased Casserole. Cover with Buttered Bread Crumbs. Bake for 25 min in preheated 375° oven.

Mrs. Walter E. Brehm
Ohio

 NOTES

Meats and Luncheon Dishes

Meats and Luncheon Dishes

Baked Barbecue Spareribs	214, 215
Baked Pork Chops	216
Baked Slice of Ham	217
Bouef Ca Vin	218
Butte Pasties	219, 220
Cheese Puff	221
Cheese Rice Ring	222
Cheese Souffle	223, 224
Chili Con Carne	225, 226
Creole Eggs	227
Damosette	228
Dinner-in-a-dish	229
Edith Barbers Sunday Night Cheese	230
Egg Cutlets	231
Egg Timbales	232
Glamorized Hot Dogs	233
Goulash	234
Green Rice	235
Ham & Vegetable Casserole	236
Ham Delicious	237
Ham Loaf with Tomato Sauce	238
Hamburger - Cheese Patties	239

Hominy Casserole	240
Hot Tomale Pie	241
Italian Delight	242
Lamb Pilaff	243
Leftover Meat Loaf	244
Macaroni Loaf	245
Meatless Dish	246
Meat Sauce for Spaghetti	247
Mexican Eggs	248
Noodle Ring	249
Nutty Eggs	250
Omelet	251
Rabbit	252
Rice & Nut Loaf	253
Rinktum Ditty	254
Spaghetti Sauce	255
Stuffed Pork Chops	256
Sweet Sour Tongue	257
Pot Roast	258
Swedish Meat Balls	259
Veal Loaf	260
Veal or Beef Loaf	261
Veal Patties	262
Venison	263
Yorkshire Pudding	264

Baked Barbecue Spareribs

To have tasty, chewy, and really delightful spareribs, that will make your family beg for more, try the following:

Select small meaty ribs; wipe with damp cloth, place in a shallow baking pan and bake in a slow oven (250°) for 2 hours, turning about every half hour. Then baste with special barbecue sauce and

(Continued)

page 2 – continued

Baked Barbecue Spareribs

and bake another half hour. Baste and turn several times.

"Barbecue Sauce"

- 3/4 C. vinegar
- 1/2 C. Prepared barbecue sauce
- 3 T. Brown Sugar
- Dash of black pepper
- Dash of red pepper
- 1/4 tsp chili powder (for "hot" sauce)

Mix together and baste ribs.

These make a delicious meal, heaped high on a platter, served with cole slaw, rye bread, fresh cherry pie ala-mode and coffee. Mmmmm Fattening? Well its worth it!

Mrs John B Sullivan – Missouri

Baked Pork Chops

5 or 6 pork chops
salt
1 can mushroom soup
milk

Brown the pork chops, season with salt and place in shallow baking dish. Stir into the mushroom soup, gradually, about an equal quantity of milk. Pour over the chops and bake in a 350 degree oven for one hour.

Mrs. George A. Dondero
Michigan

Baked Slice of Ham —

— 1 large slice of ham about one inch thick.
— 1 tsp. peanut butter.
— 2 tsp. brown sugar.
— 1 tsp. prepared mustard
— ½ tsp. clove spice or a few whole cloves.
— 3 slices of pineapple or 6 stewed prunes, or any available cooked fruit.
— 1 C. of pineapple, apple, or prune juice.

Remove rind from ham, spread with sugar, peanut butter, mustard and spice. Place in flat baking dish. Add ½ C. of fruit juice and place in preheated oven at about 450°. After about 20 minutes, lower heat to 350° and cook for about 1¼ hours more. Add the other ½ C. of fruit juice whenever necessary.

Mrs. Hal Holmes —
Washington (state)

Boeuf Ca Vin (for 6)

(This can be made in morning Reheated for dinner)

2 lbs. Chuck Beef cut in good size chunks

12 small white onions peeled, or large ones cut in quarters

8 carrots peeled and cut julienne.

8 new potatoes peeled or large ones cut in pieces, not too small or they will disintegrate

½ lb mushrooms. fresh or Dried

¼ teaspoon each of various sweet herbs Chervil, Marjoram, Rosemary savory. basil. a bay leaf.

Brown the cut up beef, onions and carrots slightly in a little butter in a heavy frying pan. If there is too much fat in the pan, pour off leaving only a nice Rich Brown Residue. Place in Deep pan or Casserole, in which you have put one clove of very finely minced garlic with other vgtables. Add herbs, Cover completely with California burgundy Cover Tightly and simmer 4 hours. Lowest possible flame. Thicken sauce with very little flour mixed with ½ cup wine There should be plenty of sauce not too thick.

Mrs. Charles S. Dewey
Illinois.

218

Butte Pasties

This recipe was probably brought from Cornwall, and the pasties were used in the lunch pails of the Butte miners. Other residents of Butte have also found them good for suppers, picnics, etc. served either hot or cold.

Plain pie dough
½ lb. raw beef steak diced
1 cup chopped onion
Salt and pepper
1 large tablespoon butter
1 cup diced rutabagas (if desired)

Pie Dough

1½ cups flour (pastry)
½ tsp. baking powder
½ tsp. salt
⅓ to ½ cup shortening
  (butter or other fat)
¼ cup cold water (about)

Sift flour, salt, and baking powder together;

Butte Pasties (cont.)

then mix, shape, roll as in directions.

For 1 pastie take ½ the dough. Roll thin, shape and size of a pie plate. Pile half the potato, onion, meat, and if desired, the rutabaga on only ½ the round of pie dough, and to within 1 inch from edge. Sprinkle with salt and pepper and dot with butter. Fold other half of this dough over this filling, press edges together well. Place 2 pasties in pie plate. Cut slit in top of each, into which a tsp. of hot water should be poured occasionally to keep from drying out. Bake ¾ hour in hot oven (400°F.) or until well browned, then reduce to 350° for 15 minutes.

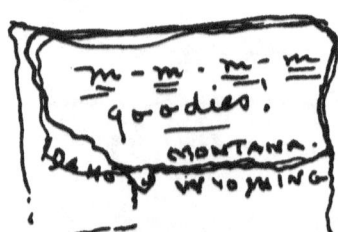

Maureen Mansfield
Missoula, Montana

Cheese Puff

1 c. ground cooked ham
1 tbsp. chopped onion
2 tbsp. shortening
2 c. soft bread crumbs
1/4 lb. Amer cheese cut fine
2 beaten egg yolks
1 1/3 c. hot milk
1/2 tsp. salt
1 tbsp. papricka
1 tbsp. minced parsley
2 beaten eggs whites

Lightly brown ham and onions in fat.
Combine crumbs, cheese yolks, milk and seasonings
Fold in stiffly beaten whites
Alternate layers of crumbs mixture with ham in greased baking dish.
Bake at 325° – 45 minutes
Serves 6

Mrs. Harlan J. Bushfield

South Dakota

Cheese Rice Ring

2 Tbsp chopped onion
1 green pepper chopped
2 Tbsp butter
1½ cups cooked tomatoes
3½ cups cooked rice
¼ tsp salt
Dash pepper
1½ cups grated sharp cheese

Cook onion and green pepper in butter until tender. Add tomatoes and rice. Cook slowly until rice has absorbed liquid. Add seasonings and cheese. Pack into buttered ring mold. Unmold into serving plate and fill with scrambled eggs.
Serves 6.

Mrs. James G. Polk
Ohio

CHEESE SOUFFLE

(Quickie!)

½# Grated American Cheese (Rat-Trap)

3. Eggs

2 cups Milk

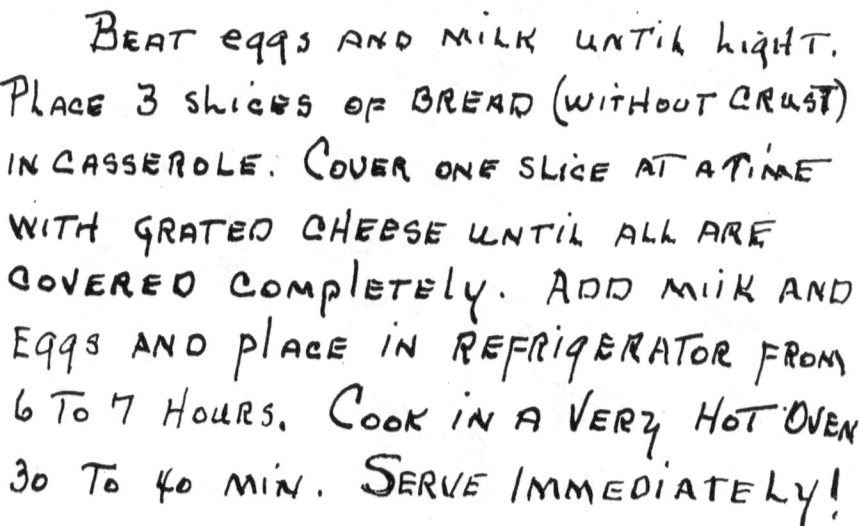

Beat eggs and milk until light. Place 3 slices of bread (without crust) in casserole. Cover one slice at a time with grated cheese until all are covered completely. Add milk and eggs and place in refrigerator from 6 to 7 hours. Cook in a very hot oven 30 to 40 min. Serve immediately!

Mrs. Clifford Davis

Tennessee.

Cheese Souffle

Two tablespoonsfuls of flour, one of butter worked together. Add One cup of sweet milk & place on stove and cook until thick white sauce; To this add one cup of grated cheese; when cool add yolks of five well beaten eggs, pinch of salt and cayenne pepper; before baking add well beaten whites folded in, bake quickly in hot oven serve at once.

— Mrs John E Rankin
Mississippi

224

Chili Con Carne

1 large onion - chopped fine
2 T butter or drippings
1 lb. round steak - ground once
1 medium can tomatoes
1 can kidney beans
2 T sugar
2 T chili powder or Worcestershire Sauce
1 tsp. salt - ½ tsp. pepper
1 T Kitchen Bouquet

Brown onion in butter in heavy iron skillet, then toss the meat in this mixture until well done. Add the tomatoes, chopped fine, and simmer slowly for 10 min. Add beans, sugar and chili powder. Cook for 15 min. longer. Add Kitchen Bouquet for color. Favorite buffet dish.

Mrs. Ralph Hunter Daughton
Virginia

Chili Con Carne

2 lbs. beef chuck　　2 tsp. salt
2 T. Chili powder　　1 onion, chopped
3 T. flour　　　　　　2 T. chopped suet
4 T. fat　　　　　　　1½ qts. hot water
　　2 cloves garlic, minced

Cut meat in small chunks, do not grind. Mix thoroughly with chili powder, garlic and flour. Melt fat and suet in large, deep pot & fry onion until tender before adding meat mixture. Cook 15 min., add salt, gradually pour on hot water. Simmer 45 min. or until meat is tender. A can of No. 1 tomato puree may be added.

TEXAS.　　　　Mrs. Paul J. Kilday

226

Creole eggs

I. Brown in butter, 5 big peppers, 2 bunches celery, 5 or 6 onions, (cut all up rather fine) When browned, add ½ gallon tomatoes, cook all until thick.

II. Make white sauce (medium) using about 1 quart milk, add 20 hard boiled eggs cut up. not to fine.

III. Use flat baking pan. Place layer of creole, layer of eggs alternately.
Bake moderate oven 30 minutes Crumbs can be used on top if you like. Serves 20.

Mrs. J. Harry McGregor
Ohio.

Damosette

2 lbs. mixed pork & beef, cubed
brown in hot fat for 10 minutes.

1 9-oz. package fine noodles
boil 8 minutes

3 large onions
1 green pepper   Chop and
4-6 stalks celery   cook together
1 can tomatoes (or fresh)   for twenty
                         minutes

Combine all above in large casserole
Add salt and pepper
    1 C sharp cheese, grated
    1 can concentrated beef broth
      (or bullion cube broth)

Bake 1-2 hours, covered

        Mrs. Walter H. Judd
          Minnesota

Dinner-in-a-Dish

4 T butter
1 medium onion chopped
2 green peppers sliced
1 lb. hamburger
1½ tps salt
¼ tps pepper
2 eggs
2 c fresh corn or canned peas
4 medium tomatoes sliced
½ c dry bread crumbs

Melt butter, sauté pepper & onion for 3 min. Add meat, salt & pepper to above & mix. Remove from fire. Stir in eggs. Mix well. Put 1 c corn (or peas) in baking dish, add ½ meat mixture, then a layer of tomatoes then repeat. Cover with crumbs. Dot with butter. Bake in 375° oven for 35 minutes.

Mrs. Ellsworth B. Buck
New York

Edith Barber's Sunday Night Cheese

6 1/4 inch slices dry bread
2 T butter or margarine
2 eggs, slightly beaten
2 C (1/2 pound) grated cheese
1 tsp. worchestershire sauce
1 tsp. salt
1 tsp. paprika
1 1/2 C milk
1/2 mustard

Remove crusts from bread. Butter bread. Line sides and bottom of shallow 1 1/2 quart casserole with bread, butter side down, cutting slices to fit. Mix salt, mustard and paprika and add eggs, milk, worchestershire sauce and cheese, stirring until well mixed. Pour mixture over bread and bake in moderate oven (350°F) 30 minutes.

Mrs. Clarence Hancock
New York

Egg Cutlets

1 T butter. ½ tsp. chopped parsley.
1 T flour. ⅛ tsp. pepper.
½ C milk. Pinch paprika.
1 tsp. grated onion. 1 tsp salt.
5 hard boiled eggs.

Melt butter, add flour & milk. Cook 'till thick stirring constantly. Add seasoning, onion & parsley, then the eggs chopped finely. Mix together & spread on plate to cool. Form in shape of cutlets, roll in bread crumbs, egg & bread crumbs. Fry in deep fat 'till golden brown, drain on brown paper, serve with Hollandaise Sauce.

Mrs. Homer A. Ramey,
Ohio

Egg Timbales

5 Eggs
1½ cups milk.
Teaspoon salt.
pepper, grated onion
chopped parsley
Beat eggs slightly
Add milk etc.
Bake in ring mold about
30 minutes in moderate oven
Serve with either cheese, tomato
or mushroom sauce. A little
sherry if mushrooms are used

Mrs. Edward Everett Laun
Kansas

Glamorized Hot Dogs

6 skinless frankfurters
1 pkg noodles
2 C cream sauce

Make a rich cream sauce
Add one tsp worcestershire
Salt and pepper to taste.
Place 1/2 cooked noodles in buttered casserole — Cut dogs in 1 inch pieces
Cover noodles — Spread on thick layer of cream sauce —
Add remainder of noodles, then rest of cream sauce.
Sprinkle generously paprika
Grated cheese and mushrooms may be added.
Bake in moderate oven 1/2 hour.
Serves 6

Mrs John H Tolan
California.

Goulash

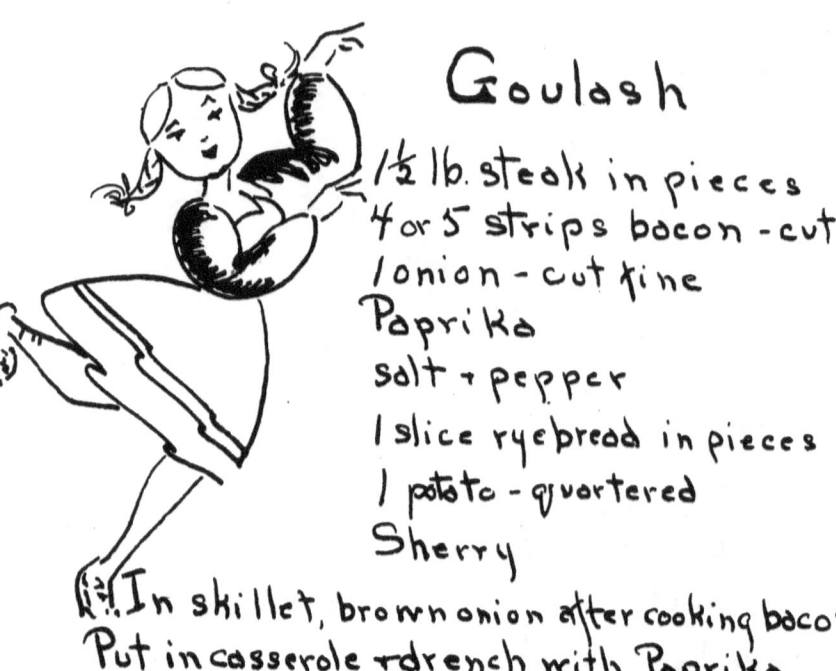

1½ lb. steak in pieces
4 or 5 strips bacon - cut
1 onion - cut fine
Paprika
salt + pepper
1 slice rye bread in pieces
1 potato - quartered
Sherry

In skillet, brown onion after cooking bacon. Put in casserole + drench with Paprika. Brown steak in skillet, salt + pepper to taste. Put in casserole, add bread pieces + plenty of Paprika. Add enough Sherry to cover, bake 45 minutes. Add potato last 20 minute of cooking.

Mrs. Thomas J. O'Brien
Illinois

Green Rice

Beat 1 egg
Add and mix well:
1 C milk
1 C finely chopped parsley
1 onion minced
2 cups cooked rice
½ C grated sharp cheese
2 T butter
salt to taste

Place in a baking dish and bake for 30 or 40 minutes in a moderate oven 325°   4 servings.

Mrs Charles A. Plumley
   Vermont

Ham & Vegetable Casserole

Fill casserole with alternate layers of
- Ground ham
- Potatoes
- Carrots
- Celery

Sprinkle generously with parsley, season to taste with salt and pepper. Cover with mushroom soup. Cook in moderate oven for about an hour and a half

Mrs. Chet Holifield
California

Ham Delicious

Soak ham in cold water for one day, then simmer slowly the second day, do not let it come to a boil. The third day it must remain in its own juices. The fourth day it is skimmed, covered with "sugar and spice and all that's nice" and put in the oven and browned. The result is worth the labor.

        Mrs. William C. Burgin
        North Carolina

Ham Loaf with Tomato Sauce.
2 lb. pork steak } grind together
1 lb. ham
2 eggs
1½ C. milk
1 C. mashed potatoes
1 onion (grated)
　　Bake at 325° - 1½ hours.
　　　　Sauce
½ C. vinegar
½ C. butter
2 tsp. prepared mustard
3 egg yolks
½ C. sugar
½ C. cream of tomato soup.
dash of salt.
　　Melt butter in double boiler. Beat egg yolks in a bowl and add sugar and vinegar. Add this to the melted butter, then the tomato soup, mustard and salt. Beat well and cook until thick.

　　　　Mrs. August H. Andresen
　　　　　　Minnesota.

Hamburger-Cheese Patties

2 lbs. ground beef
1 C. grated cheese
1 C. stuffed green olives
½ C. bread crumbs
½ C. milk
1 egg
1½ tsp salt
pepper
2 T. worchestershire sauce.

Mix to-gether and form into patties. Wrap with a piece of bacon and stick with toothpick. Bake in 375° oven for an hour. This can be made into a loaf with bacon on top.

Mrs. Walt. Horan
Washington

– Hominy Casserole –

1 lb. ground beef
1 can hominy
3 lg. onions diced
1 bell pepper
¼ tsp. chili pepper
1 can tomatoe sauce

Fry onion and bell pepper until tender. Add ground beef, cook. Add hominy, seasoning, tomato sauce. Put in baking dish.
Cream sauce – Melt 2 T butter, add 2 T flour, 1 C. milk, ½ C. cheese. Cook until thickened. Pour over beef mixture, sprinkle top with cheese. Bake 35 min., 350° oven.

Mrs. Albert E. Carter
California

Mrs. Edouard Victor Izac
San Diego California.

Hot Tamale Pie

2 cups ground cooked meat
½ cup tomatoes (canned or fresh)
1 cup gravy or meat stock
1 tablespoon chili powder
1 teaspoon salt — ½ small garlic clove minced
1 qt. cooked mush very stiff.
Mix meat with gravy, chili powder, salt and garlic. Line baking dish sides and bottom with cold mush. Fill with meat mix, put mush over top in broken pieces Garnish with California ripe olives.
Bake from 20 to 30 minutes in hot oven.

Italian Delight.

2 lbs. ground meat
½ lb. American cheese, grated
10¢ package cooked egg noodles
no. 2 can cream corn
no. 2 can Heinz tomato soup
1 tbs. butter
salt and pepper
1 large onion
garlic, if desired

Cook onion slowly in fat, add meat and cook until it is no longer red. Keep stirring. Add tomato soup and corn. Add noodles and cheese in layers. Heat twenty minutes in a casserole.

Mrs. O. Clark Fisher.
Texas.

Lamb Pilaff

1 Leg of Lamb – 6 Cloves of Garlic

Make incisions in surface of lamb and insert 5 or 6 peeled cloves of garlic. Place lamb, fat side up, in roasting pan. Sear in oven at 500 degrees. Reduce heat to 325 degrees, and cook thirty minutes to the pound.

One hour before lamb is to be served, pour 3 cups of boiling water into the pan, and add 1 cup of washed rice. Serve lamb with rice surrounding it. With green salad makes 1 dish meal.

Mrs. Robert A. Taft, Ohio

Leftover Meat Loaf.

3 cups ground left-
  over meat, any kind.
1 cup bread crumbs
  or 2 slices bread
    soaked in milk
    or water and
    crumbled.
  or leftover potatoes
Add any leftover vegetable.
1 good sized onion chopped.
1 egg (optional).
Salt; pepper; ½ teaspoonful
  of poultry dressing.
Shake of catsup, chili or Worcestershire sauce, or A-1 sauce.
2 teaspoonful butter, or beef
  or bacon grease
Water to make firm loaf.
Put in greased pan in oven
  for 30 minutes.
Use hot or cold.

      Mrs. John C. Schafer,
        Wisconsin.

Macaroni Loaf

½ C. macaroni
½ C. cheese
1 C. soft bread crumbs
1 C. milk
2 T. minced onion
2 T. minced parsley or pimento
¼ C. oleomargarine
3 eggs   salt and pepper

Boil macaroni in salted water, and drain. Add to bread crumbs chopped onion and parsley. Put milk in double boiler, scald until cheese is melted, add oleomargarine, and beaten egg yolks. Pour over mixture, stir all together, and season well. Fold in beaten whites of eggs. Bake one hour in buttered tin, in pan of water.

Serve with mushroom sauce -- cream sauce, with sautéd mushrooms added.

Mrs. John W. Heselton
Massachusetts

Meatless-day dish.

Cook 2 C macaroni until tender while you prepare the following sauce.

Partly fry 1 large onion in 3 tablesp. butter or margarine. Add 2 chopped green peppers and 1½ C tomatoes or tomato juice. Cook for 15 minutes. Add 1 C. grated cheese. ½ teaspoon sage and 1 teaspoon of salt. Also pepper to taste. Bake in buttered casserole dish for 30 minutes. More juice may be added if desired.

Mrs. A. M. Fernández
New Mexico

Meat Sauce for Spaghetti

1 LB ground beef
½ LB ground lean pork
1 Can tomatoes
2 Cans tomato Paste
1 Can tomato Puree
1 large onion chopped fine.
1 Can Pimento
1 Garlic Button

Sear beef and Pork until no red shows.
Fry onion and pimento.
Put meat, onion and pimento in pot with tomatoes, paste and puree and simmer slowly for several hours.
Serve on Spaghetti.

Mrs. Robert Ramspeck
Georgia

247

Mexican Eggs

2 T Celery
2 T Cabbage
2 T Head Lettuce
1 tsp Onion
4 T Chili Sauce

Cut fine and place in heavy skillet. Simmer five minutes.
Add
2 T Sherry

Drop 4 whole Eggs onto mixture. Cover and cook slowly until Eggs are set. Serves four.

Mrs Kenneth S. Wherry
Nebraska

Noodle Ring.

1 pkge. egg noodles (broad) — 1 tsp. salt
2 eggs — 2 T cheese grated
½ C. rich milk or cream; mushrooms or chicken creamed.

Boil noodles in salted water for 20 minutes; drain; add eggs, milk or cream, salt and grated cheese; place in well buttered mold; bake in moderate oven until set; place creamed mushrooms or chicken or both in centre to make a complete dish.

   Mrs. H. P. Kopplemann,
     Connecticut.

Nutty Eggs

1 doz cooked eggs
1/2 cup chopped blanch almonds
1 tsp Worcesterchire sauce
Very small amt garlic.
Salt and Pepper.

Split eggs, remove yolks
and cream with mayonnaise
add nuts and seasoning
Refill eggs with mixture
Dash with paprika.

   Mrs John H. Tolan
    California.

Omelet
Service 2 or 3

3 eggs
pinch salt and pepper
3 T. cream or milk

Separate 3 eggs; add to yolks a pinch of salt and a little pepper; beat until light; add 3 tablespoons of cream or milk; beat the whites stiff and fold into the mixture; pour into a hot buttered frying pan and cook about 2 minutes over the flame; put into hot oven about 1 minute; serve immediately.

Mrs. Owen Brewster
Maine.

Rabbit

California Style

1 good sized rabbit
1½ tsp. salt
⅛ tsp. pepper
⅓ C. flour
1 section garlic
3 T butter or savory
    drippings
2 C. heated milk
½ C. sour cream.

Coarse boiled hominy
Pickled pears or Crab apples

Dress the rabbit. Scrub, rinse thoroughly with fresh water, dry + disjoint. Mix salt, pepper + flour + roll rabbit pieces in it. Peal the garlic + rub the inside of a heavy frying-pan. Melt the fat in pan + brown rabbit in it. Place in a casserole, pour in the milk, cover + bake 40 minutes or until tender at 350-375°. Last add the sour cream. Serve with coarse hominy + garnish with pickled pears.

Mrs. Norris Poulson,
California.

Rice & Nut Loaf

2 C pecans or walnuts, chopped
2 C cooked rice
1 C dry bread crumbs
1 C milk
1 beaten egg
1 T flour
2 T butter or margarine
Chopped green peppers & celery
Salt & pepper

Mix chopped nuts, rice & bread crumbs. Add milk, egg, flour & butter. Add peppers, celery & seasoning to taste. Mix well into loaf, pack tightly in a well greased pan. Bake for 1 hour in moderate oven (325-350 degrees) Serve with mushroom or tomato sauce.

Substitute for meat dish

Mrs Frank Carson
Kansas

Rinktum Ditty

1 can tomato soup
2 c. cheese (strong) diced
¼ t. soda
1 c. milk
2 eggs (beaten)
Salt, pepper, cayenne

Heat tomato soup in double boiler. Add cheese. When blended add soda, milk, eggs. Season.

Serve on saltines. Eat while hot.

Also good for sandwiches.

Margaret Chase Smith
2nd District Maine

Spaghetti Sauce

1 lb. round steak
  (ground or cut.)
1 large can tomatoes
3 large onions
1 clove garlic

Cook tomatoes, onions and garlic until well done, strain, using juice only. Fry meat in 2 T. mazola oil. Add meat to juice. Add 1 handful dry or canned mushrooms.
Add 3 cans Del Monte tomato sauce. Season with salt, red pepper and Worcestershire sauce. Cook until thick. This is to be served over spaghetti that has been cooked 20-30 min. Sprinkle with grated cheese, preferably Parmesian.
This sauce can be prepared a day ahead and serves 6 people generously.

Mrs. R. Ewing Thomason,
Texas.

Stuffed Pork Chops

6 - 1 inch pork chops
2 C. toasted bread crumbs
2 T. butter
1 small onion
Cream — enough to moisten dressing
Salt + pepper to taste
2 T. chopped green pepper

Slice chops in middle to bone. Fill with dressing made from other ingredients. Bake in slow oven about 1½ hr.

"Boy, am I ever stuffed!"

Mrs. Willan C. Cole
Missouri

Sweet Sour Tongue

1 fresh beef tongue
2 Bay leaves
1 onion
1 tsp. salt
2 T. vinegar

Something Good To Eat

Boil together between 2 or 3 hours. Remove skin and save water for sauce

Sauce

1 T. butter
2 T. flour
1 C. raisins

Juice of 1 lemon
¼ C. red wine
Sugar to taste

Brown flour in butter, strain water from boiling tongue into flour + butter, add remaining ingredients. Slice tongue + put it in the sauce. Let come to a boil and simmer a few minutes.

Mrs Wm H. Link
Illinois.

Pot Roast

- 5 lbs Beef Pot Roast
- 1 Med. Onion Chopped
- ¼ C. Bacon Drippings
- 2 T. Salt
- 2 T. Parsley Chopped
- 1 1½/2 Can Tomatoes - or 4 C. Tomato Juice
- 1 C Flour
- 1 Clove Garlic
- 4 T. Sugar
- 1 Tsp. Pepper
- 1 Bay Leaf

Wipe Meat with damp cloth. Pound in as much Flour as Meat will hold. Insert Garlic (which has been peeled and quartered) in Meat. In Dutch oven heat drippings and Sauté Onions until transparent but not brown. Remove Onions to Mixing Bowl. Plunge Meat into hot oven and brown thoroughly on both sides about 10 to 15 minutes per side. Add remaining ingredients to sautéd onions pour over brown meat and let come to a boil. Roast 45 minutes per pound. Turn every hour. Add water if moisture is required. Serve in squares with the pan gravy.

Mrs. J. Buell Snyder   Penna.

"Swedish Meat Balls."

1 lb. ground beef.
1 large onion, minced.
1 C. cracker crumbs.
1 egg. Salt + pepper.

Mix and make into balls. Brown in fairly deep bacon fat. Pour can of cream of mushroom soup over balls, also ½ can of water. Cover. Simmer for one hour.

Mrs. Homer A. Rainey,
Ohio.

Veal Loaf

1½ # veal } ground together
¾ # pork

½ c. milk
1 " bread crumbs
2 eggs
½ onion
¾ tsp. salt
pepper

Bake slowly in covered dish for two (2) hours. Put strips of bacon on top.
Good if served with mushroom sauce made of juices in pan.

Mrs. W. Sterling Cole
New York

Veal or Beef Loaf

2 1/2 lbs. of ground veal or beef
1/2 lb.   "   "   pork
2 eggs
3/4 C of bread crumbs
1 C milk
1/2 of an onion chopped
pepper   salt

Soak bread in milk while preparing other ingredients. Fry 1/4 lb. bacon which has been cut in pieces and add to the mixture.

Tomatoes or mushrooms may be added.

Mrs. J. Roland Kinzer
Pennsylvania

Veal Patties

1 lb. ground veal
4 T bread crumbs
1 can tomato paste
2 cans water
1 T. vinegar
1 tsp. sugar
¼ tsp. basil
Pinch of soda
1 tsp. poultry seasoning
1 tsp. onion juice
1 tsp. Worchestershire sauce
Salt + pepper to taste.

Make patties of veal, bread crumbs, salt + pepper + brown well in greased iron skillet. Add other ingredients, cover and simmer 40 minutes. Serve with rice.

Mrs. S. W. Arnold
Missouri.

Venison

-Roast-

In roast of venison, lard meat by cutting small slits several inches apart then inserting pieces of bacon or pork fat in slits. Salt and pepper the meat well. Place in roasting pan, add ½ C water and garlic bud. Cover pan. Roast at 325°, 30 minutes to each pound. Add water as needed.

-Fried-

Cut venison leg or loin in thin slices Salt and pepper well. Pound flour in. Fry quickly in bacon grease.

Mrs. Mayme Morse
Oregon

Yorkshire Pudding
served with Roast Beef.

4 eggs
2 C. milk
1 C. flour
½ tsp. salt
1 tsp. baking powder

Beat eggs and add milk. Add salt, baking powder to flour. Stir dry ingredients into milk and eggs, stirring until smooth. Pour into meat drippings around the roast + bake 30 to 40 minutes in quick oven. Will serve six.

Mrs. J. Will Robinson
Utah.

Pastry Index

Never Fail Pie Crust.	267
Pie Crust.	268
Banana Cream Pie.	269
Chocolate Pie.	270
Date Cream Pumpkin Pie.	271
Eggnog Pie.	272
English Apple Pie.	273
Fresh Peach Pie.	274
Fresh Peach Meringue Pie.	275
Graham Cracker Cream Pie.	276
Lemon Chiffon Pies.	277, 278
Lemon Pie.	279
Lime Meringue Pie.	280
Mississippi Pecan Pie	281
Pecan Pies.	282, 283
Pumpkin and Marmalade Tarts.	284
Rhubarb Pie.	285
Whipped Lemon Pie.	286, 287
Nesselrode Pie.	288

Never Fail Pie Crust

½ C. Shortening
¼ C. boiling water
1½ C. flour
Pinch of Salt

Put shortening in bowl and add boiling water. Stir until shortening is melted. Stir in the flour to which the salt has been added. Form in ball & allow to sit in refrigerator at least 3 hours.

This amount will make 2 pie shells.

Mrs. Joseph W. Ervin
North Carolina

Pie Crust

2 c flour 1/4 t salt
2/3 c shortening cold water

Sift together flour and salt. Cut in shortening with two knives or shortening cutter. Add cold water very slowly and just enough to blend mixture together. Divide mixture. Roll each half very lightly on floured board. Amount will make one double pie or two single pies.

Mrs. Dean P. Taylor
New York

Banana Cream Pie

1 1/3 c milk
3 1/2 T flour
2 egg yolks
2/3 t vanilla
2/3 c sugar
2 T butter
2 bananas

Mix the sugar and flour in the upper part of double boiler; beat eggs; add milk; add liquid gradually to the sugar mixture; drop in the butter and place over hot water, stirring as it thickens; cook for 20 minutes. When cool add vanilla and pour into baked crust in alternate layers with sliced bananas. Cover with meringue, brown in a moderate oven.

Mrs. Robertson
Wyoming

"And the moon was a big round pie." Selected

Chocolate Pie

3 T. cocoa
3 T. flour
2/3 C. sugar
1 C. milk

3 eggs - separated
Pinch of salt
1 T butter

Blend together cocoa, sugar + flour, add milk. Beat egg yolks + add milk enough to make 1/2 cup. Add to blended mixture + cook in double boiler until thick enough to separate in bottom of pan. Add salt + butter. Pour into a baked pie crust and cover with meringue.

For meringue use whites of 3 eggs and beat until fluffy. Add 3 T sugar, pinch of salt + 1/4 tsp. vanilla.

Bake in oven 15 minutes at 250°.

Mrs. Lyle H. Boren
Oklahoma

Date Cream Pumpkin Pie

2 C. Pumpkin pulp
3/4 C. sugar
2 T. flour
1/2 tsp. salt
1 tsp. ginger
1 tsp. Cinnamon

2 Eggs, beaten
2 C. milk, scalded
1 C. cream, whipped
Dates

Mix pumpkin, dry ingredients, scalded milk & beaten eggs; pour into pie shell; bake at 350 °F, for about 1 hour. Serve with whipped cream; dot with diced dates. A meringue may be used instead of whipped cream.

Lillian Gronna Herbert.
North Dakota.

Eggnog Pie

1 C. milk
1/4 tsp. nutmeg
3 egg yolks
1/2 C. sugar
1/8 tsp. salt

1 T. gelatin
1/4 C. cold water
1 tsp. vanilla
3 egg whites

Heat milk in double boiler & add nutmeg; beat egg yolks, sugar & salt together; add to milk stirring constantly; cook until mixture coats the spoon; soak gelatin in cold water; add to custard & cool; add flavoring & fold into stiffly beaten egg whites; pour into a crust (either a baked pie shell or graham cracker crust). Top with whipped cream & grated chocolate. Chill well.

Mrs. Alexander Wiley
Wisconsin

English Apple Pie

Peel, core and slice 5 or 6 medium sized apples and pack firmly in a small baking pan, cover with ½ cup of granulated sugar and sprinkle heavily with cinnamon.

In a small mixing bowl knead one cup brown sugar, ¼ cup of flour and 1 stick of butter. Pat out and spread over apples for crust. Bake 45 minutes in medium oven.

Serve with whipped cream.

Mrs. Oscar E. Bland,
Indiana.

Fresh Peach Pie

Peach 1/2's.

3/4 c. sugar.
3 T. flour.
1 tsp cinnamon.
3/4 c. coffee cream.
Pecans.

    Arrange the peaches in the unbaked pie shell, cut side down. Mix sugar and flour—sprinkle over the peaches.

    Pour the cream on top and sprinkle with pecans and cinnamon.

    Bake at 450° for 10 mins. to bake crust. Then 350° for 30 to 45 mins. Best served warm.

Mrs. Carl T. Curtis
Nebraska

Fresh Peach Meringue Pie.

2 cups very ripe peaches diced.
1 T. flour.   Dash of salt.
2/3 cup sugar.
2 eggs.
1 baked pie shell.

#

Mix peaches, sugar, flour and egg yolks until syrup forms. Cook on low fire until juice thickens but peaches are not cooked. Pour into pie shell and cover with meringue made of egg whites and ¼ cup sugar. Brown lightly.

Mrs George W. Gillie
Indiana.

Graham Cracker Cream Pie

12 Graham Crackers rolled
1/8 Pound butter or oleomargarin
1/2 C sugar
Mix to form dough Press firmly into pie plate
Bake 10 minutes

Cream Filling

Use 1 box Jello Vanilla Pudding Make according to instructions on box. When thickened add 2 egg yolks well beaten with 1 Tb. milk.

Use egg whites to make meringue for top.

Mrs. Everett P. Scrivner
Kansas

Lemon Chiffon Pie

5 eggs 5 T. lemon juice
3/4 C Sugar 1 T. Butter

Beat egg yolks & add lemon juice, also sugar. Cook in Double Boiler until thick. Keep stired. When done add butter & let Mixture Cool. Then fold in two beaten egg whites, & use remaining 3 egg whites, beaten on top of pie.

Mrs Victor Wickersham,
Oklahoma.

Lemon Chiffon Pie

4 Eggs – Separated
3/4 Cups Sugar
4 T. Lemon Juice
1 T. Butter

Cream egg yolks and sugar thoroughly, add lemon juice. Cook in a double boiler until thickened, stirring often. Add butter; remove from fire and fold in stiffly beaten whites of two eggs. Pour into baked pie crust, cover with a meringue made from the remaining egg whites stiffly beaten, with four tablespoonfuls of sugar added. Brown meringue in a slow oven 350° F. for fifteen minutes. This makes one eight inch pie.

Mrs. Martin L. Smith
(Washington)

Lemon Pie

3 T. cornstarch
1 C. sugar
1 lemon
3 eggs
Pinch of salt
1½ C. boiling water

Mix together cornstarch, sugar and salt. Cover with grated rind and juice of lemon. Add beaten yolks of eggs, then add boiling water and cook until thick. Pour into baked pie shell.

Beat egg whites until stiff but not dry. Gradually beat into them 3 T. sugar. Spread over the top of the lemon mixture. Bake in slow oven (350°F.) fifteen minutes or until meringue is light brown.

    Mrs. Earl R. Lewis
     Ohio.

Lime Meringue Pie

- ½ C. water
- 5 T. cornstarch
- 1½ C. milk
- 1¼ C. sugar
- 4 egg yolks beaten
- 1 T. butter
- Juice of 4 limes
- Grated Rind of 1 lime
- 1 baked 9-inch pie shell

Mix ½ C. water + cornstarch to thin paste. Combine milk + sugar in top of double boiler. Bring to boil over direct heat. Add cornstarch paste + boil until the mixture begins to thicken, stirring constantly. Return to double boiler + continue cooking until thick + smooth (15 minutes). Stir occasionally to keep smooth. Pour in beaten egg yolks + cook two minutes longer. Add lime juice, butter, + lime rind. Mix well. Cool and pour into pieshell. Top with meringue made of the beaten egg-whites, 4 T. sugar, a few drops of vanilla + grated rind of ½ lime. Brown in 325°F. oven.

Mary Barbara Cole
Missouri

Mississippi Pecan Pie

3 whole eggs

3/4 cup brown Karo syrup

3/4 cup sugar

Mix eggs, sugar, and syrup. Cook mixture in double boiler until thick. Then pour in baked pie crust and cover with pecans. Brown in oven for a second. Watch closely for the pecans are easily burned.

Miss Annie Laurie Rankin
Mississippi

Pecan Pie

3 eggs
1 cup whole pecans
1½ C dark Karo syrup
1 T soft butter
½ tsp vanilla
⅓ C brown sugar
1 T cornstarch

Method

Mix all ingredients and bake in unbaked pie shell in hot oven (425°) for 10 minutes. Lower temperature to (350°) and bake 40 minutes. Serve with whipped or ice cream.

Mrs Wm. Lemke
North Dakota

Pecan Pie

1 C brown sugar
3/4 c dark Karo syrup
3 eggs
1 tsp vanilla
1 cup pecans
2 T butter

cream butter and sugar add syrup and well beaten eggs, then the other ingredients. Bake in an uncorked pie shell in a moderate oven until firm

Mrs. Geo. Mahon
Texas

Pumpkin and Marmalade Tarts

3 eggs slightly beaten
1 C. sugar
1 tsp. salt
½ tsp. each cinnamon, nutmeg and ginger
¼ tsp. cloves
2 C. strained, cooked pumpkin
2 C. milk scalded

Combine ingredients in order given. Line tart pans with pastry. Place 1 tsp. orange marmalade in bottom of each shell. Fill with pumpkin mixture.
Bake in hot oven 10 minutes; reduce heat to 350° and bake until filling is set and pastry lightly browned. Serve topped with whipped cream and decorate with a cherry.

Mrs. Edward G. Rohrbaugh
West Virginia

Rhubarb Pie

2½ c. rhubarb
¼ tsp. salt
1¼ c. sugar
⅓ c. flour
2 eggs
1 tbsp. butter

Cut rhubarb in half inch pieces. Mix sugar, flour and beaten eggs. Add rhubarb. Pour in unbaked pie crust and cover with lattice strips. Bake at 375° for twenty minutes, then reduce heat to 325° until done.

IOWA — Mrs. Thomas E. Martin
Iowa

Whipped Lemon Pie

1 tsp. Knox Gelatine
1/4 c. cold water
4 egg yolks
1/2 c. sugar

Dash salt
2 lemons
1 c. cream
2 tbs sugar

Combine 4 egg yolks beaten with 1/2 cup sugar. Add dash salt. Add juice and grated rind of the 2 lemons. Cook in double boiler until thick, stirring constantly. Add gelatine which has been soaked in 1/4 c. cold water for five minutes, stirring until gelatine is dissolved. Allow to cool and partially set. Beat 4 egg whites until stiff adding 1/2 c. sugar slowly while beating. Whip 1 cup cream with 2 tbs. sugar. Mix whipped cream with stiffly beaten egg whites and fold into lemon mixture. Turn into baked pie crust and top with whipped cream and nut meats, if desired. This recipe can also be used for a pudding and served with angel food cake. Makes medium sized pie, or eight individual servings in sherbet glasses

Helen Gahagan Douglas

NOTES

Simplest Nesselrode Pie

Soak 1 envelope Knox Gelatine in ¼ c. cold water.

Scald 1 c. cream and 1 c. milk.

Mix in saucepan: ¼ c. sugar, 1 t. salt, + three egg yolks. Pour scalded milk slowly over last mixture. Return to stove + cook until it coats a spoon (stir constantly). Remove and add gelatine. Stir until dissolved - then place aside to cool.

Whip 3 egg whites stiff - Add ⅓ c. sugar + about ¼ t. vanilla. When custard is cold, but *not set* fold in egg white mixture. Pour into pastry shells + place in refrigerator to cool. Before serving, grate bitter - sweet chocolate on top!

Mrs. Joe L. Evins
Tennessee

Pickles and Preserves Index.

Bar-Le-Duc	291
Chili Sauce	292
Green Tomato Mincemeat	293
Kosher Dill Pickles	294
Mothers Favorite Pickles	295
Peach Conserve	296
Quick Orange Marmalade	297
Rhubarb Conserve	298
Seven Minute Preserves	299
Yellow Tomato Preserves	300

Bar-le-duc -

4 cups sugar
1 " water
Boil 10 min.
add 1 qt. stemmed currants
Boil 8 min. more
Let stand a few hours and
seal cold.

This is delicious served
with Philadelphia Cream
cheese and crackers as a
dessert.

Mrs. Dow Harter
Ohio

Chili Sauce

½ Bu. peeled Ripe Tomatoes
½ "   "   " Peaches
5 Large Onions
3 or more Red peppers } Chopped

4 T. Salt
16 T. Brown Sugar
1 T. Cinnamon
2 T. Celery seed
2 T. White mustard seed
50 whole cloves

Boil slowly 3 hrs.
When nearly done add 6 c. vinegar
Bottle + seal.

Mrs. Jay LeFevre
New York

Green Tomato Mincemeat

12 C. green tomatoes } chopped
12 C. tart apples
3 lbs. raisins
8 C. brown sugar
2 C. suet – chopped fine.
1 pt. cider
2 T. salt
2 T. cinnamon
1 tsp. nutmeg
1 tsp. cloves

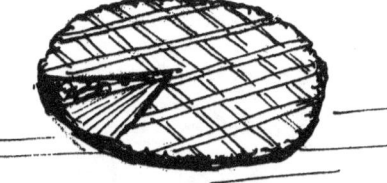

Drain juice from tomatoes + add same amount of water. Scald + drain – Do this 3 times, then add raisins, sugar, salt + suet. Cook until clear. Add spices, apples + cider. Cook until thick.

Put in jars and seal.

Mrs. Augustine B. Kelley
Pennsylvania

Kosher Dill Pickles

20-25 dill-sized cucumbers
1/8 t. powdered alum
1 clove garlic
2 heads dill
1 hot red pepper
1 quart vinegar
1 c. salt
3 quarts water
grape leaves

Wash cukes; let stand in cold water overnight. Pack in sterilized jars. To each quart add alum, garlic, dill red-red pepper. Combine vinegar, salt and water; bring to boil; fill jars. Place grape leaf in each jar and seal. Makes 6-8 quarts.

Mrs. H. Sterling Cole
New York

— Mother's Favorite Pickles —

Two quarts very small cucumbers.
Two quarts very small onions.
Two quarts pieces of cauliflower.
8 or 10 green peppers cut up.

<u>Mix</u> all together, then put into weak brine. Let stand <u>24</u> hours. Take out of brine and drain. Cover with new brine. Scald and drain well.

<u>Mix</u> to a smooth paste with a little cold water, the following:—
  ½ C. mustard.
  4 C. sugar.
  1 C. flour.
  2 T. curry powder.

<u>Heat</u> to boiling point two quarts of vinegar, add paste, stirring constantly. Boil up well and pour over vegetables. Seal in small glass jars.

Mrs. Hal Holmes
Washington

Peach Conserve

2 Oranges sliced thin
1 Cup pineapple
6 Cups sugar
2 Peach seeds
2 Cups water
5 cups sliced peaches
1 cup maraschino cherries sliced

Cook oranges in the water 1 hour. Fix peaches and 4 cups sugar and let stand ½ hour. Put peaches, pineapple and oranges together and cook ½ hour. Add 2 cups sugar and cherries and cook ½ hour.

Mrs. Frank A. Barrett
State of Wyoming.

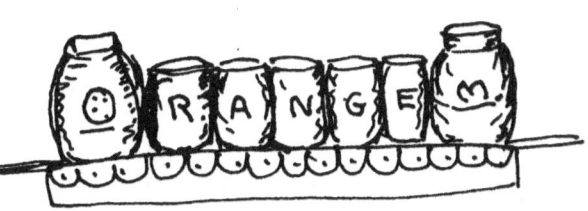

Quick Orange Marmalade.

4 Oranges   4 Lemons

Wash fruit and with a sharp knife cut it into very thin slices, thin as paper. To every pint of pulp add three pints of water - let this stand over night. In the morning cook one hour, cool. To every pint of cooked fruit add a pint of sugar. Boil the mixture until it jellies from a spoon. Pour marmalade into clean hot glasses and cover with paraffin when cold.

  Mrs. Dwight L. Rogers,
   Florida.

Rhubarb Conserve

4 pounds rhubarb
4 pounds sugar
1 pound raisins
2 oranges
1 lemon

Orange peelings cut fine, and juice, Lemon rind grated and juice. Rhubarb cut in small pieces. Put all together let stand one hour. Cook slowly for 45 min.

Mrs. Ross Rizley
Oklahoma

Seven Minute Preserves
(Strawberry)

Wash & stem berries. Drop 1 packed box into a pan of boiling water. As soon as the water boils up in them, skim out, & put into another pan.

Add 1 C. sugar & 1 T. lemon juice. After it begins to boil, cook 3 minutes. Then add ¾ C. sugar & cook 4 minutes from time it starts to boil.

Pour into large pan. Add each batch as it is finished. Let them stand over night. In the morning pack (cold) in sterilized jars & cover with wax. Cook only 1 box at a time. Use slow heat.

Mrs. Lowell Stockman
Oregon

Yellow Tomato Preserves

4 lbs. yellow pear tomatoes
4 lbs. sugar
½ lb. preserved ginger - sliced
4 lemons - sliced

Cover tomatoes with boiling water until skins slip off easily.
Add sugar + let stand overnight.
Pour off liquid + boil until thick, skim. Add tomatoes, ginger + lemons. Cook slowly until tomatoes become translucent and syrup thick.
Seal in hot jars.

Mrs. Augustine B. Kelley
Pennsylvania

Salads

Salads Index

Avocado Salad	304, 305
Cabbage Relish Salad	306
Celery Salad	307
Cheese Salad	308
Cheese & Tomato Salad	309
Cherry Salad	310
Chicken Salad	311
Cranberry Salad	312
Egg Ring Salad	313
Evalyns Salad	314
Fresh Fruit Salad	315
Fruit Salad	316
Green Bean & Cheese Salad	317
Guacamole Salad	318
Jellied Apricot Salad	319
Macaroni Salad	320
Maurice Salad	321
Pineapple & Carrot Salad	322
Quick Tomato Aspic	323
Stuffed Head Lettuce Salad	324
Tuna Fish Mold	325

Salad Dressings

Avacado Salad Dressing	326
Cooked Fruit Salad Dressing	327
French Dressing	328, 329
Honey Dressing	330
Honey Salad Dressing	331
Hot Sauce Tartare	332
Russian Dressing	333
Mustard Sauce	334, 335

Avocado Salad

1 package Lemon jello
1 cup boiling water
1 cup sour cream (heavy)
1 cup mayonnaise
1 cup mashed avocado

Mix jello and hot water. When cool add other ingredients. Garnish with quartered tomatoes and watercress, or lettuce.

Mrs. R. Ewing Thomason.
Texas.

Avocado Salad

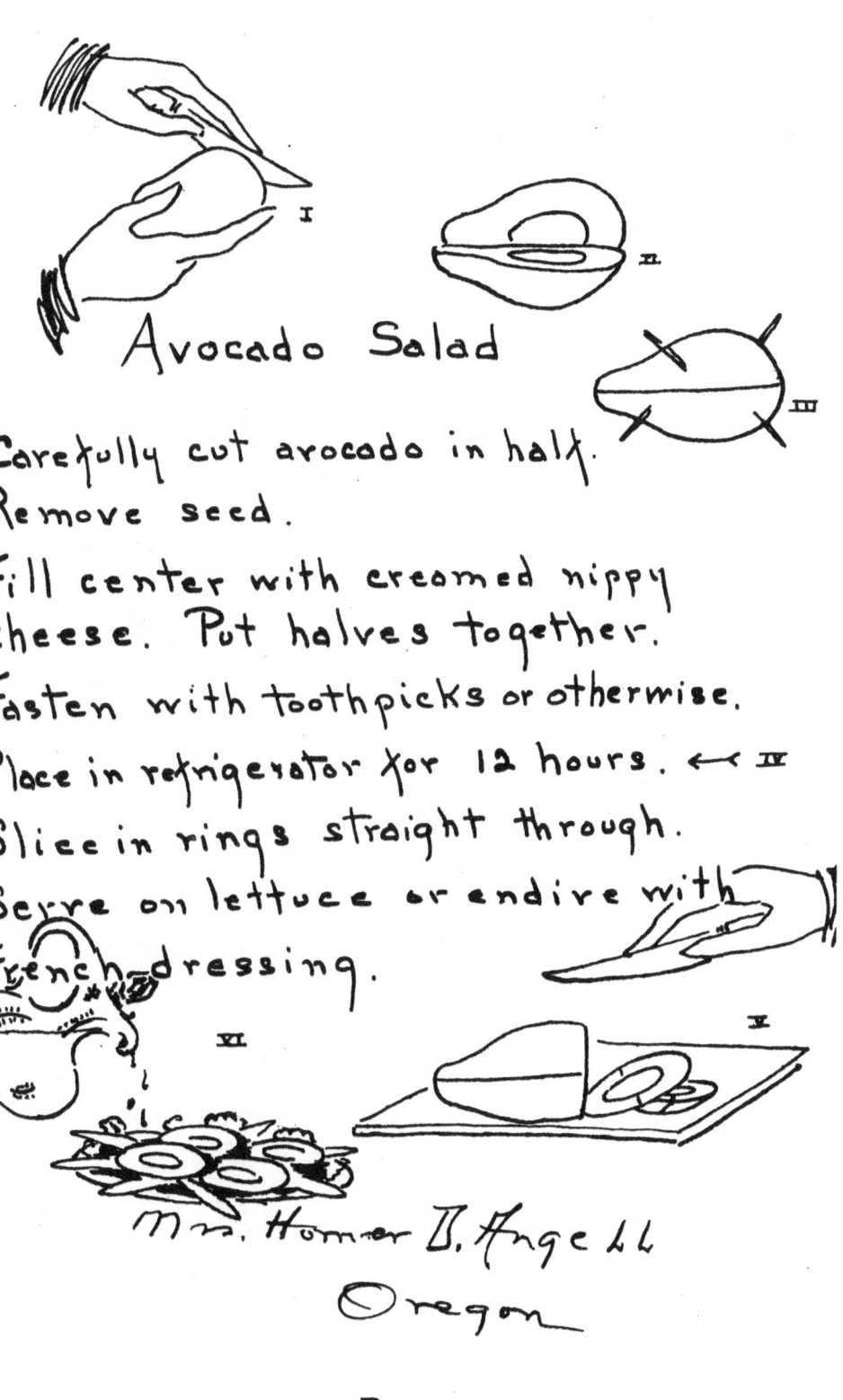

Carefully cut avocado in half.
Remove seed.
Fill center with creamed nippy cheese. Put halves together.
Fasten with toothpicks or otherwise.
Place in refrigerator for 12 hours.
Slice in rings straight through.
Serve on lettuce or endive with French dressing.

Mrs. Homer D. Angell
Oregon

Cabbage Relish Salad

- 3 cups shredded Cabbage
- 1 cup canned Red Kidney Beans
- ½ cucumber, diced
- ½ Green pepper, shredded
- ⅓ cup diced celery
- 1 Table sp. minced onion
- ¾ Tea sp. salt
- ½ cup Vinegar
- ⅛ Tea sp. Paprika
- ½ cup cream

Crisp cabbage, cucumber, celery in iced water. Drain as dry. Blend all ingredients together except cream and chill in refrigerator. Just before serving stir in Cream. Also very good made with a French dressing —

Mrs Albert H. Hawkes -
New Jersey —

Celery Salad

- 2 C Celery cut in small pieces
- 2 C Diced apples
- ½ C Diced sweet pickles
- ½ C Chopped walnuts
- ¼ tsp Salt
- ½ C Mayonaise

Mix well. Chill, serve on lettuce.

Mrs. Luther Patrick
Alabama

Cheese Salad

2 packages cream cheese moistened by 2 T. cream.

Chop fine
1 c. cherries
½ c. walnuts
4 slices pineapple
½ green pepper

Whip 1 c. cream and 1 c. mayonnaise together

Add salt and paprika

Pack in freezing tray

Freeze stiff and slice.

Margaret Chase Smith
2nd District Maine

Cheese & Tomato Salad

1 can tomato soup
½ can water
3 cakes Phila. cream cheese
½ cup each chopped celery, nuts
   and green pepper
1 Cup mayonnaise dressing
2 T. sp. gelatine dissolved in
½ cup cold water
Salt and red pepper to taste.

———————

Heat soup, add cheese, let melt, add gelatine; let cool, add mayonnaise + other ingredients; mold and serve on lettuce with mayonnaise.

Makes 12 to 16 individual molds.

Mrs. S. Otis Bland
Virginia
309

Cherry Salad.

1 package jello (cherry)
1 c. boiling water
1 can dark, sweetened cherries and juice
1 c. chopped celery (if desired)
1 c. chopped pecans.

Mrs. O. Clark Fisher.
Texas

Chicken Salad

1 - 4 pound chicken
Cook and dice chicken
add the following
1 C diced celery
3/4 C pimento olives
1 C pecans or almonds
4 hard cooked eggs diced
Salt to taste
1/2 C salad dressing

Dressing

4 egg yolks whipped to lemon color
1 C salad oil
Juice of one lemon
2 tsp vinegar
1 tsp dry mustard
1 tsp salt
few grains cayenne
1/2 tsp sugar

Mrs Karl Le Compte
Iowa

Cranberry Salad

1 quart cranberries
2 cups sugar
2 oranges

Cook together, then add 2 tablespoons gelatine. Cool and add one cup nuts and one cup celery.

Mrs. Frank A. Barrett
Wyoming.

Egg Ring Salad

6 hard boiled eggs (put thru ricer)
1 T. gelatin
1/2 C. cold water
1 C. boiling water
1 onion (grated)
1 bunch parsley (chopped)
2 T. mayonnaise
1 T. vinegar
salt, pepper, paprika

Soak gelatin in cold water add boiling water then other ingredients which have been mixed together. Pour into ring mould, chill. Turn out on bed of lettuce, fill center with lobster, chicken or shrimp salad.

Mrs. Charles R. Clason

Massachusetts

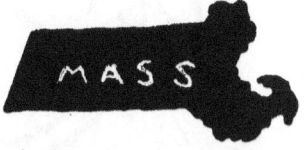

Evalyn's Salad

lettuce
ripe olives
artichoke hearts
beets - tiny whole } canned
asparagus tips
French dressing

Aw, g'wan "You all",
use your artistic sense
and serve.

Glessie M. O'Neal
(Mrs. Emmet O'Neal)
Louisville, Ky.

Fresh Fruit Salad

1. Flute the edge of half an orange shell and fill with mayonnaise decorated with slices of maraschino cherries
2. Two kinds of melon balls — green and yellow color
3. Sections of orange and grapefruit
4. Mound of cottage cheese .. paprika
5. Fresh raspberries and blueberries
6. Half of peach .. filled with jam
7. Cherries
8. Slices of orange
9. Sections of banana rolled in nuts
10. Decorate with chickory and mint leaves.

Mrs. Charles Clason
Massachusetts

Fruit Salad.

1 can fruit salad
½ can Black cherries and all the juice in can.
½ c mayonnaise
1 c whipped cream
2 envelopes Knox gelatine (plain)

Soak gelatine in enough cherry juice to dissolve it. Bring rest of cherry juice to a boil + let cool, then add soaked gelatine. Add blanched almonds + all other ingredients + pour in mold. Serve with mayonnaise on top

Mrs Albert Thomas
Texas

Green Bean & Cheese Salad

INDIANA

I.
- 1 can French green beans
- 1 t. Lea & Perrins
- juice of ½ lemon
- salt
- ½ small onion

II.
- ⅓ lb Phil cream cheese
- handful pecans
- ½ small onion
- salt
- 2 t mayonaise

III.
- 1 envelope gelatin
- ¼ cup cold water
- ½ cup boiling water

Add half of Part III to Parts I & II — mix well — put Part I in mold first then Part II

Mrs Charles LaFollette
Indiana
317

Guacamole Salad
Avocado

2 avocados, mashed
1 onion, minced
1 tsp. lemon juice
1 tsp. chili powder
1 tomato, chopped fine
1 T. salad oil

Combine ingredients, season to taste with salt and pepper.

Use as a salad or as hors d'oeuvre.

Mrs. Paul J. Kilday
Texas.

Jellied Apricot Salad

1 large can whole peeled apricots
1/3 c. peanut butter
1/4 c. chopped nuts
1/4 c. chopped dates
juice 1 lemon
1 pkg. lemon jello
2 c. hot water

Remove pits from drained apricots. Combine peanut butter, nuts and dates with lemon juice, mix well. Fill the cavity of each apricot with a spoonful of this mixture, press halves together. Put one filled apricot in each individual mold. Fill mold with jello which has been chilled.

Mrs. Lawrence Smith
319 Wisconsin.

Macaroni Salad

- 1½ C Short length macaroni
- 2 C Chipped celery
- ½ C Sweet relish or diced pickles
- ¼ C Chopped onion
- ¾ C Walnuts
- ½ C Mayonaise
- 2 Tbs. Lemon juice
- 2 Hard boiled eggs
- Salt and pepper

Cook macaroni in salted boiling water, drain and blanch. Add celery, pickles, onions, walnuts, salt and pepper. Mix mayonaise and lemon juice add to salad and mix lightly. Chill, serve in lettuce-lined bowl. Garnish with sliced eggs and walnuts.

Mrs. Luther Patrick
Alabama

Maurice Salad

2 heads Lettuce - shred
1 C. cooked chicken - cut in strips
2 C. baked or boiled ham - cut in strips
3 T. chopped pickle
3 or 4 tomatoes - cut small.

Mix well, add Dressing, toss + garnish.

Dressing

3 T. finely chopped onion
3 hard boiled eggs - chop
3 T. mayonnaise
3 T. olive oil
2 T. vinegar
1 tsp. Worcestershire Sauce

Mrs. Wm. E. Hess
Ohio

PINEAPPLE AND CARROT SALAD

2 grated carrots
1 medium sized can shredded pineapple
2 envelopes Knox's Gelatine
3/4 cup juice left from spiced fruit

Drain pineapple.
To the pineapple juice add the spice and enough water to make a pint.
Heat to boiling and pour over gelatine which has been dissolved in a little cold water.
Cool. When it starts to thicken add pineapple and grated carrot.
A diced cucumber may be added if desired.
Pour into moulds, place in refrigator to harden.
When ready to serve, turn out on lettuce leaf and serve with mayonnaise.

Mrs. Robert F. Rich,
Pennsylvania

PINEAPPLE - CARROT - SALAD!!!

Quick Tomato Aspic

Dissolve
1 can of condensed Tomato Soup
in
1 package of Strawberry gelatine

Add
1 Tsp. of horse radish
A pinch of marjoram

Pour
in ring mould — chill

Serve
with filling of cottage cheese
and chives

Garnish with watercress

Mrs. Ralph Church
Illinois

Stuffed Head Lettuce Salad

Remove core from lettuce wash and drain well.

Mix 2 packages Philadelphia Cream Cheese with chopped onions - olives - garlic - pimentoes or anything you wish for flavoring.

Press cheese mixture into lettuce head through core opening, getting it in as far as possible.

Wrap in wax paper and put in refrigerator until thoroughly chilled.

When serving cut in quarters, sixths or eighths instead of slicing.

Mrs. Paul Shafer
Michigan

ONE SIXTH, PLEASE!

324

Tuna Fish Mold

2 Envelopes of gelatin
1 Cup chicken broth
1 Can Tuna fish
½ Cup celery
½ Cup blanched Almonds
½ Can (No 2) green peas with juice
½ Cup mayonnaise
2 chopped eggs
Juice of one lemon

Scald Tuna fish, mix all ingredients and add melted gelatin
Pour in Pyrex loaf dish and let harden. Garnish and slice.

Mrs. Robert Ramspeck
Georgia

Mrs. Edouard Victor Izac
San Diego - California.

Avocado Salad Dressing.

1 teaspoon salt
1 teaspoon pepper
1 teaspoon dry mustard
1 teaspoon Worchestshire sauce
1 teaspoon onion juice
1 teaspoon horseradish
½ cup sugar
2/3 cup vinegar
1 cup Wesson oil
½ to 2/3 cup tomato soup

Mix all together in glass quart jar and shake well before using.

This is very fine for all kinds of salad and keeps indefinitely in ice box.

COOKED FRUIT SALAD DRESSING

½ Cup sugar.
½ tsp salt.
1½ tbl's flour.
1 well beaten egg.
½ Cup pineapple juice and
¼ Cup orange juice.
2 tbl's vinegar.

Combine in order given, and cook in double boiler stirring constantly until thick. Cool.

Mrs. John M. Baer.

NORTH DAKOTA

French Dressing

1 cup salad oil
1/4 cup vinegar
1 1/2 tsp. paprika
1 tsp. salt
1/2 tsp. onion juice
1 tsp. dry mustard
1 tsp. wokchestershire sauce
1 T. of. tomato cat sup
1/2 cup sugar

———————

Beat oil and vinegar well with dover beater. Mix dry ingredients and add; beat well; add orange + lemon juice + other seasoning. Keep in glass jar in refrigerator.

Mrs. S. Otis Bland
Virginia

French Dressing

- 1 C salad oil
- ¼ C vinegar
- ¼ C catsup
- 1 tsp. salt
- 1 C sugar (scant)

Use egg-beater to mix above ingredients; then add juice of one-half lemon and beat again. Keep in covered jar in refrigerator.

Mrs. Geo. A. Dondero
Michigan.

Honey Dressing

"Grand; for fruit salads. There's just enough tart- and -sweet to tease and enhance"—

2/3 c. sugar
1 tsp. dry mustard
1 tsp. paprika
1/4 tsp. salt
1 tsp. celery seed
1/3 c. strained honey
5 tbsp. vinegar
1 tbsp. lemon juice
1 tsp. grated onion
1 c. salad oil

Mix dry ingredients; add honey, vinegar, lemon juice, and onion. Pour oil into mixture very slowly, beating constantly with rotary beater. Makes 2 cups. Soak celery seed in water 2 hours; drain.

Mrs. Jed Johnson
Oklahoma

Honey Salad Dressing

½ Cup honey
½ Cup catsup
½ Tablespoon mustard
½ Tablespoon paprika
1 Teaspoon sugar
1 Teaspoon salt
1 Kernel garlic
1½ Cup Salad oil

Beat well — and add the salad oil very slowly with vinegar to taste.

Frances P. Bolton M.C.
22nd Ohio District

Hot Sauce Tartare.

1 tablespoon butter.
1 tablespoon flour.
½ cup milk.
⅓ cup mayonaise.
1 shallot finely chopped.
½ tablespoon capers finely chopped
1 teaspoon vinegar.
½ tablespoon pickles finely chopped.
½ tablespoon olives finely chopped.
½ tablespoon parsley finely chopped

Make a white sauce with flour and milk.
Add various ingredients, stir constantly until mixture throughly hot
Add dash of cayenne.

Mrs Charles S. Dewey
Illinois.

Russian Dressing

½ cup sugar
1 tsp. salt
1 tsp. paprika
⅓ tsp. cinnamon
½ tsp. cloves
1 tbsp. A1 sauce
¼ cup vinegar
⅔ cup catsup
1 cup oil (salad)
juice of 1 lemon

Mix dry ingredients. Add others. Mix with egg beater.

Maureen Mansfield
Missoula, Montana

Mustard Sauce
for Vegetables or Ham

⅓ C. vinegar
½ C. tomato soup
½ C. prepared mustard
½ C. sugar
⅓ C. margarine
3 beaten egg yolks

Mix first 3 ingredients in a bowl. Cream last 3 in double boiler. Combine + cook, stirring constantly until it thickens. Serve hot or cold over vegetables or meat. Will keep in icebox.

Mrs. George Outland
California.

Mustard Sauce

½ C sugar
2 tsps mustard (dry – Coleman's)
½ C vinegar
1 C cream
1 T flour

Mix and cook in double boiler until thick.
Serve hot over meat. Can be used cold.

Mrs Charles A. Plumley
Vermont.

Soups – Index

Clam Chowder	339
Clear Tomato Soup	340
Cold Tomato Soup	341
Cream of Lettuce Soup	342
French Onion Soup	343
Hawaiian Crabmeat Soup	344
Mock Turtle Soup	345
Mushroom Soup	346
Old Fashioned Vegetable Soup	347
Onion Soup	348
Rhode Island Chowder	349
Scotch Broth	350
Split Pea Soup	351
Vichysoise	352

Clam Chowder.

1/4 lb. salt pork, diced.
1/2 C. onions, diced.
4 C. potatoes, diced.
2 C. cooked clams.
T. butter.
Salt & pepper.

Fry salt pork & onions together.
Boil potatoes & drain. Cover with milk, add clams, salt, pepper & butter. Blend with salt pork and onion mixture, heat & serve.

Mrs. Homer A. Ramey,
Ohio.

Clear Tomato Soup

2 No. 2½ cans solid pack tomatoes
1 large onion
1 large sprig parsley
1 whole egg beaten
2 egg shells
ice
1 pt. veal stock
2 qts. water
salt to taste.

Mix tomatoes, onion, parsley, egg and shells. Add a piece of ice as large as a lemon. Add the stock which has been skimmed. Cook until onion is done. Add the hot water and salt. Serve with a thin slice of tomato in the bottom of each bowl.

Mrs. John S. Wood — Georgia

Cold Tomato Soup

2 cups beet juice - canned or raw.
2 large cans of tomatoes ⎫
1 onion   ⎬ Simmer ½ hour
few stalkes of celery
a little parsley
1 c water   ⎭

Strain + chill.
Peel 2 cucumbers - dice & soak in ice water - no salt.
Mix a tart French Dressing. Mix beet juice - tomato juice - add enough French Dressing to flavor well. Season with salt & pepper to taste. Put a small lump of ice into this just before serving and beat until oil is well mixed. Serve at once with a T. of cucumber and T. of sour cream in each plate.

   Mrs. Dow Harter
     Ohio

341

Cream of Lettuce Soup

1/4 lb. of butter
1 1/2 quarts unskimmed milk
6 leaves of good firm lettuce
3 medium sized onions
          chopped fine

Use double boiler. Melt butter then add lettuce & onions. Cover & let cook 45 minutes. Add one heaping cooking spoon of flour. Add milk & stir until very smooth & slightly thickened. Salt & pepper.

        Mrs. C. Douglass Buck
            Delaware

French Onion Soup
Serves 6

6 onions
4 T butter
1 scant tsp. salt
2 C water
2 cans consommé
Dash Kitchen Bouquet

Shred onions; sauté in melted butter. Mix all ingredients + simmer 3 hrs. Toast bread slices in 2 inch squares. Sprinkle with grated cheese, toast in broiler + serve one in each soup bowl.

Mrs. Harold H. Burton
Ohio.

Hawaiian Crabmeat Soup
"Quickie"

1 can condensed tomato soup
1 can condensed pea soup
1 C. thin cream or top milk
½ lb. crabmeat

After thoroughly heating, add ¼ C sherry.
Serve immediately.

Mrs. Joseph Rider Farrington
Hawaii

Mock Turtle Soup

- 1 Beef Tongue
- 1/2 Can Tomatoes (strained)
- 1/2 C Flour (browned in oven)
- 1/2 Tps. Ground Cloves
- 1/2 Tps. Allspice
- 3 Large Potatoes
- 2 Hard Boiled Eggs
- 1/2 Lemon cut in small pieces

Boil tongue until tender, remove from liquor and skin. Cut small end of tongue into little pieces. Return liquor to kettle and add strained tomatoes. Add spices to flour, add enough cold water to make a thin paste, add to broth. Heat and let boil well. Add meat.

Pare and cut potatoes in dice, boil until tender.

Before serving put a spoonful of the boiled potatoes, a couple slices of hard boiled egg and several pieces of lemon in each soup plate add hot soup. Serve immediately.

Mrs. Robert F. Rich,
Pennsylvania

Mushroom Soup

¼ lb. mushrooms
1 medium onion
2 T butter
1 T flour
¼ t pepper
½ t celery salt
1 t salt
4 C. milk

Peel and grind mushrooms and onions. Cook in butter in double boiler 10 min. Add flour and seasonings. Add milk gradually. Cook 20 min.

Serve at once, or store in glass jar in icebox until needed.

  Mrs. Edward R. Burke
   Nebraska

Old-Fashioned Vegetable Soup

2 lb. soup bone or left over bones
4 qts. water.
　　　　Boil ½ hour.
Grind in meat chopper and add to soup.
　　4 white potatoes
　　4 onions
　　1 green pepper
　　4 stalks celery
　　4 carrots

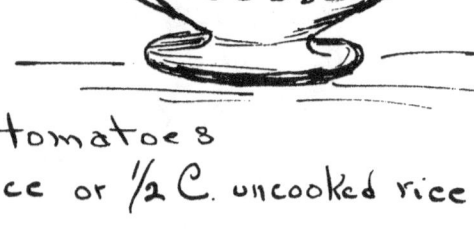

Add - 2 C. stewed tomatoes
　　　2 C. cooked rice or ½ C. uncooked rice
　　　1 Bay leaf
　　　Salt and pepper to taste.

Cook slowly 2 to 3 hours. Add water if necessary. Remove bones and Bay leaf and serve.

Mrs Albert H. Hawkes
New Jersey

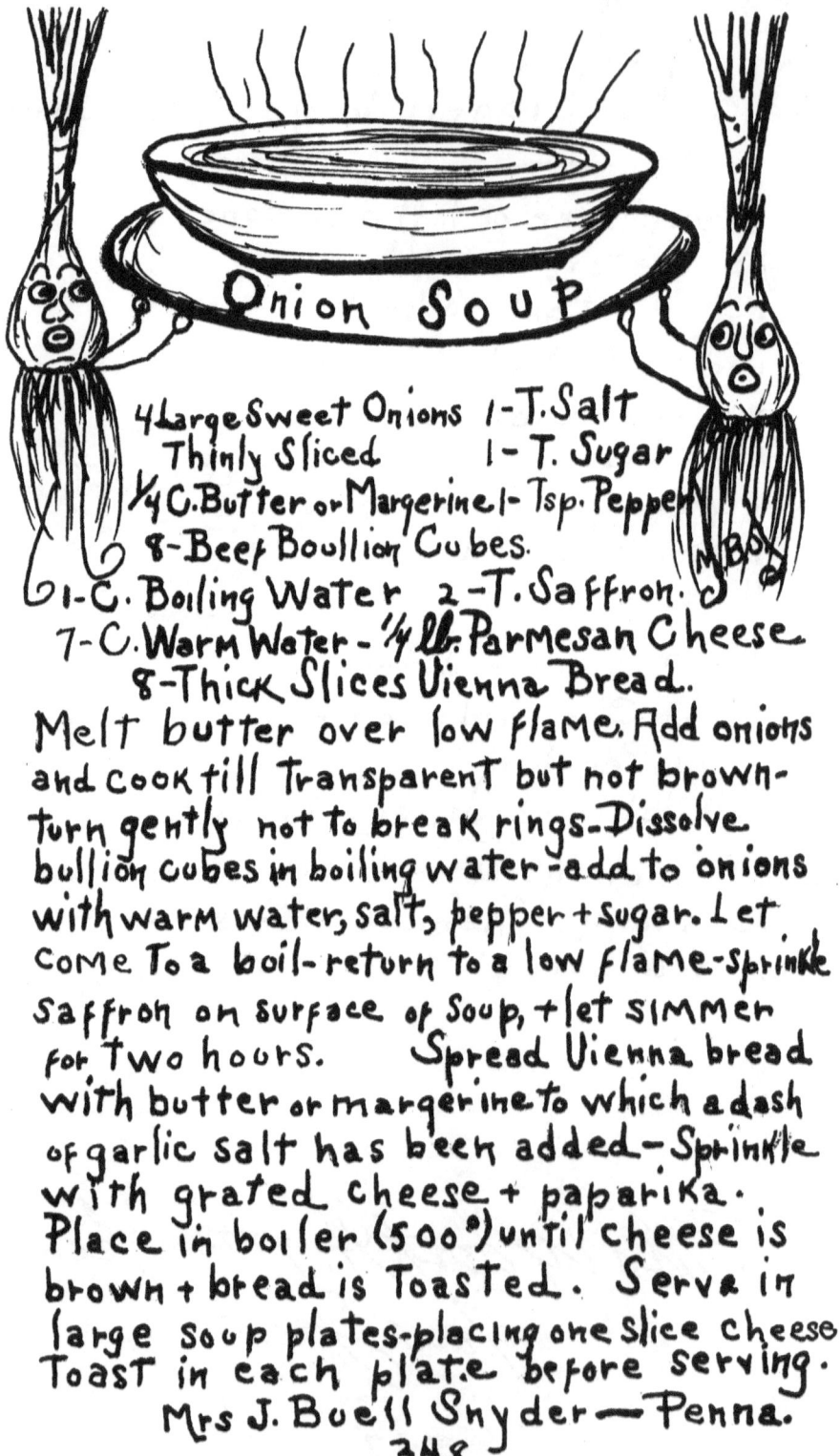

Onion Soup

- 4 Large Sweet Onions Thinly Sliced
- 1-T. Salt
- 1-T. Sugar
- ¼ C. Butter or Margerine
- 1-Tsp. Pepper
- 8-Beef Boullion Cubes
- 1-C. Boiling Water
- 2-T. Saffron
- 7-C. Warm Water
- ¼ lb. Parmesan Cheese
- 8-Thick Slices Vienna Bread

Melt butter over low flame. Add onions and cook till transparent but not brown- turn gently not to break rings. Dissolve bullion cubes in boiling water - add to onions with warm water, salt, pepper + sugar. Let come to a boil - return to a low flame - sprinkle saffron on surface of soup, + let simmer for two hours. Spread Vienna bread with butter or margerine to which a dash of garlic salt has been added. Sprinkle with grated cheese + paparika. Place in boiler (500°) until cheese is brown + bread is toasted. Serve in large soup plates - placing one slice cheese toast in each plate before serving.

Mrs J. Buell Snyder — Penna.

Rhode Island Chowder

Get two slices of salt pork, then melt in saucepan. Fry 1 onion in this fat, add 2 raw potatoes diced, add water to cover potatoes, then add 1 can tomato soup & cook till potatoes are done.

Shortly before serving add 1 pt. of chopped quahogs.

Season to taste with salt and pepper.

Mrs. Aimé J. Forand
Rhode Island

Scotch Broth
(From a Scotch Family)

1 small white turnip
2 medium carrots
1/4 head cabbage (Kale)
4 large onions (leeks)
All put through food chopper.
1 can peas
1 cup pearl barley
1 cup rice
1 large beef shank
Salt and pepper to taste

Cook all together except peas, which are added last. May be kept in cold place and reheated as needed.

Mrs. Daniel G. Reed
New York.

Split Pea Soup

Cook in salted water till tender 3 C. split peas.

Simmer beef bone to get 2 qts. of stock.

Cook the following with the beef bone + stock —

4 stalks celery, 4 onions, 4 carrots, 8 bay leaves, 1 garlic bud, 1 clove, ½ tsp. poultry seasoning, ½ tsp. thyme, pinch red pepper, salt + pepper.

Remove beef bone + press it all through a sire.

Makes about 8 bowls of soup.

Mrs. Lowell Stockman
Oregon

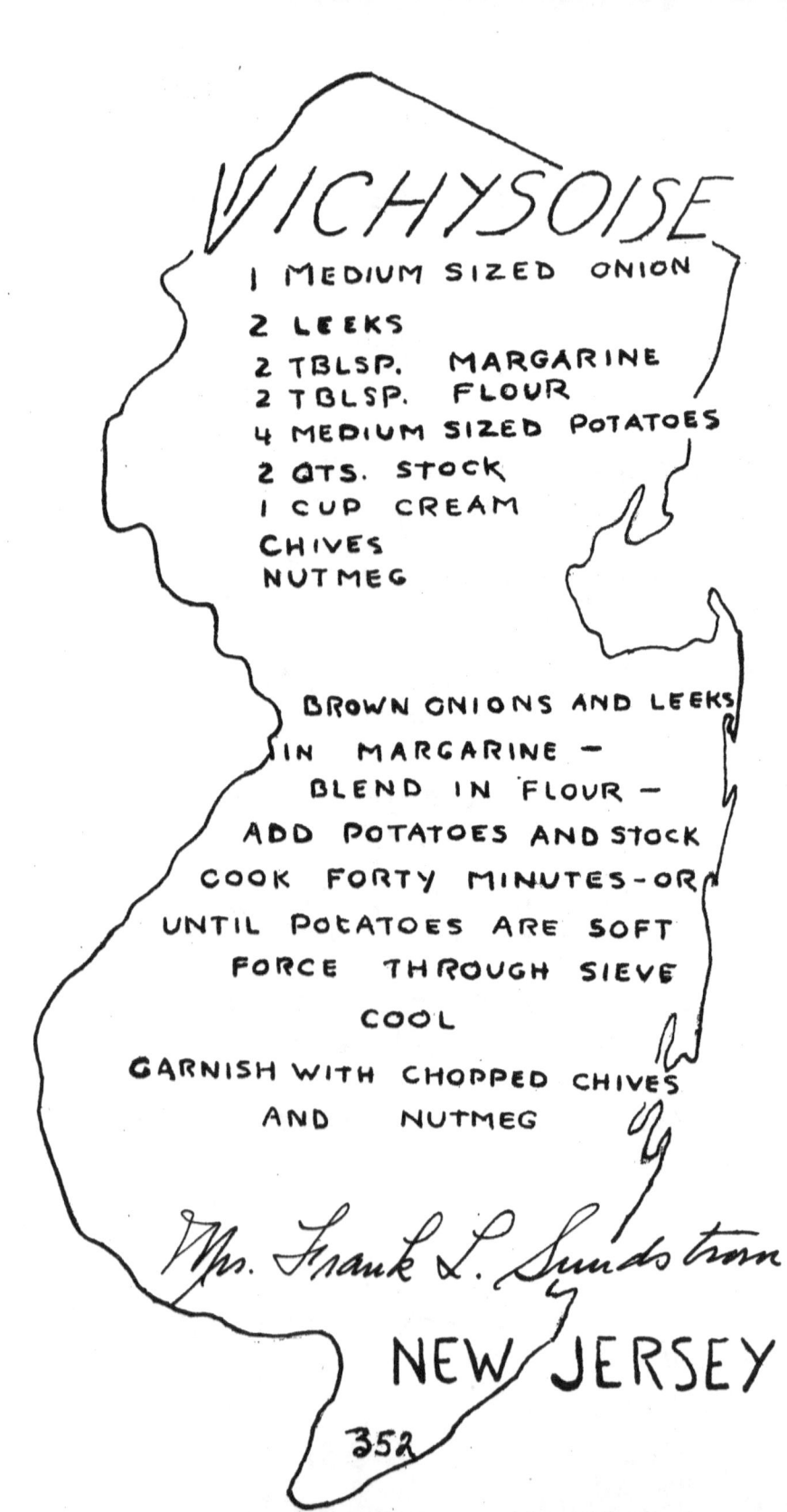

Vegetable Index

Almond and Asparagus Casserole	355
Appled Sweet Potatoes	356
Baked Beans	357
Baked Curried Onions	358
Stuffed Cabbage	359
Baked Cabbage Roll	359
Cabbage Au Gratin	360
Caraway Cabbage	361
Carrot Loaf	362, 363
Delicious Corn Cakes	364
Cauliflower with Almonds	365
Egg Plant Souffle	366
French Peas	367
Green Rice	368
Harvard Beets	369
Idaho Potato	370
Idaho Potato Piglets	371
Onion Pie	372
Spanish Peas	373
Stuffed Peppers	374
Sunshine Carrots	375
Sweet Potato Baskets	376
Tomato Creole	377
Vegetable Scallop	378
White House Dish	379

Almond And Asparagus Casserole

1 can (green or white) asparagus tips
1/4 lb yellow cheese (cut in strips)
1/2 lb blanched almonds
2 cups Cream Sauce
1 cup bread crumbs

Line a buttered baking dish with asparagus tips. On this place cheese, then almonds. Cover with cream sauce, then another layer of tips, cheese, and almonds, more cream sauce, and top with bread crumbs. Bake in moderate oven for 30 minutes.

Mrs. Pete Jarman,
Alabama

"Appled" Sweetpotatoes

Slice the sweetpotatoes.
Dice the apples.
Butter the casserole.
Arrange layer of sweetpotatoes
— salt, pepper, butter.
Add layer of apples
— sugar, nutmeg. (Be generous.)
Repeat the above layers.
Bake in moderate oven.

Mrs. John R Murdock
Arizona

Baked Beans

Soak 2 c. beans overnight. Drain off water and cover with cold water to which ¼ t. soda has been added.

Parboil about ½ hr. Turn off water. Rinse with cold water. Add 3 T. olive oil, 2 in square, salt pork, 2 t. salt, 1 t. mustard, ½ t. ginger, ¼ t. red pepper, 1 T. molasses, 1 onion.

Cover all with hot water. Let stand over low heat for ½ hour. Place in oven, covered. Bake slowly 250° for 8 hrs.

Keep covered with water.

Margaret Chase Smith
2nd District Maine

Baked Curried Onions

5 large onions
3 T butter
2 tsp flour
Few grains Cayenne pepper
1 tsp Curry powder
1 T beef extract
1 C milk
½ C grated cheese (yellow)

Put thinly sliced onions into saucepan with 1 sp. water. Cover & simmer until tender.

In a double boiler blend butter, flour & seasonings. Add beef extract & stir in milk gradually.

Add cheese, reserving some for top of dish.

Stir constantly until mixture is thick.

Place onions in buttered baking dish, cover with sauce, then grated cheese. Bake in moderate oven for 30 minutes.

Mrs Christian A. Herter
Massachusetts

— Stuffed Cabbage —

Remove heart from the head of cabbage, stuff with pork sausage which has been seasoned. Place in a double boiler (allowing no water to touch cabbage) and cook for two hours. When ready to serve, place on platter and pour over it a rich white sauce.

Mrs. Albert H. Vestal
Indiana

— Baked Cabbage Roll —

Parboil a head of cabbage in salted water. When cool, take off each leaf.

Mix together 1 pound pork sausage, 1 C. boiled rice, 1 diced onion, 2 raw eggs. Season to taste.

Fill each cabbage leaf with the meat mixture and pin with a toothpick. Brown in frying pan, then place in casserole and bake for 30 minutes. Left over meat, ground, may be substitued for sausage.

Vivian Vestal
Indiana

Cabbage au Gratin

1 small head cabbage
½ C. American cheese
2 Ts butter

2 Ts flour
1 C. milk
½ tsp salt

Cut cabbage into small pieces. Cook in salted water 8 min. or until transparent; drain well; place in baking dish; add cheese sauce made as follows: blend melted butter & flour; add milk & salt; cook until thickened, stirring constantly; add grated cheese & stir until cheese is melted. Bake ½ hr. at 350°.

Mrs. Alexander Wiley
Wisconsin
HOME, SWEET HOME.

Caraway Cabbage

1 medium head cabbage - shredded
  Cover with boiling water in covered kettle while preparing: —
3 medium onions, sautéed
  Add 1 tsp. caraway seed and 1 tsp. salt.
  Drain cabbage, add onions and cook slowly for three minutes or until all moisture is gone.
  Mix 1 T flour, 2 T sugar, and ½ C vinegar.
  Stir into cabbage and cook until thickened.

Mrs Paul Shafer
Michigan

— Carrot Loaf —

2 C. cooked, mashed carrots
1 diced onion   } Boiled together
1 diced green pepper }   + drained.
3 eggs, beaten separately.

— Sauce —
4 T. butter
4 T. flour
½ C. milk
Salt + pepper

Add sauce to vegetables.
Add egg yolks. Fold in egg whites.
Pour into buttered casserole.
Bake in oven at 350-400° for 45 minutes.

Mrs. Norris Poulson
California

Carrot Loaf

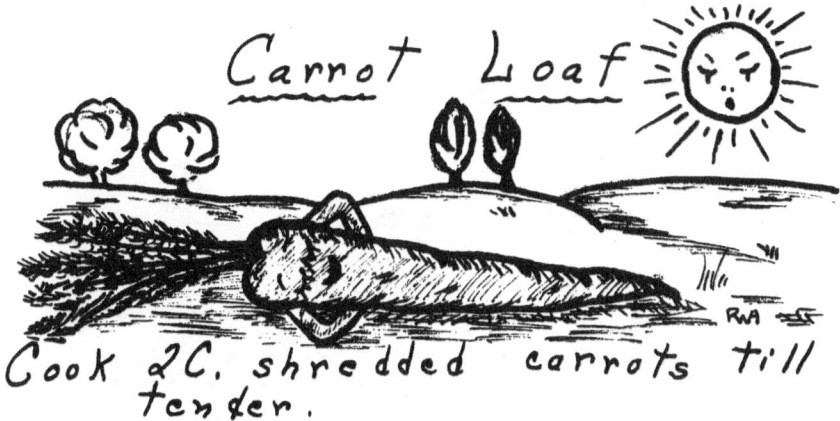

Cook 2 C. shredded carrots till tender.

Drain & save ½ C. liquid, to which add ½ C. milk or cream & 1 C bread crumbs.

Grate 1½ C. of cheese.

Beat 2 eggs.

Fold all together & bake in a buttered dish in a pan of water for 1 hour at 375°.

Serve with a crab, tuna or mushroom sauce.

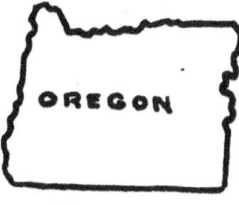

Mrs Lowell Stockman
Oregon

Delicious Corn Cakes

1 doz. ears raw corn, scored + pulp pressed out with back of knife. Do not allow any skins to get mixed in pulp.
3 eggs beaten separately
1 tablespoon of flour

Mix thoroughly. Put butter in skillet + when bubbling drop corn mixture from spoon + fry until quite brown.

Mrs. C. Douglass Buck
Delaware

Cauliflower with Almonds

1 - Medium head of Cauliflower
1 - handful salted Almonds
1 C. White sauce.
Paprika or Grated Cheese

Trim leaves from Cauliflower leaving 1 inch of stem for support. Add hot water to cover stem but not touching head; Cover and steam until tender, about 25 minutes. Cut off stem and place in a serving dish. Stick almonds around in Cauliflower or chop and sprinkle over top, then pour over white sauce, sprinkle with cheese or paprika.

Mrs. Laurence Smith
Wisconsin

Eggplant Souffle

1 medium eggplant. Peel, slice and boil in salted water until tender. Chop fine when done.

1 T butter
3/4 C milk
1 C bread crumbs
1 onion, chopped fine.
2 eggs well beaten.
Salt and pepper to taste.

Put in well greased baking dish alternating bread crumbs with other mixture.

Cover top with grated cheese and buttered crumbs. Bake in moderate oven 30 to 40 min.

Mrs. Hugh Peterson, Georgia.

FRENCH PEAS

4 slices of bacon, diced.
1 small onion, minced.
1 c. cream.
2 c. canned peas.

Sauté the bacon and onion in a skillet until the bacon is crisp, and the onion is yellow. Drain the fat, add the cream, and the drained peas. Salt and pepper to taste. Simmer until the cream is thickened.

Chopped parsley and pimentoes add color. Makes 4 to 6 servings.

Mrs. Carl T. Curtis
Nebraska

Green Rice

½ C. olive oil
Fry 1 onion and
½ clove of garlic
in the oil.

1 C (uncooked rice) cooked and cooled –

1 heaping C. grated cheese
1 heaping C. parsley cut fine
1 C. milk
2 eggs beaten together
Salt.

Mix altogether and bake in 350° oven for 45 minutes. This is delicious served with creamed shrimp, crab or chicken.

    Mrs. Leroy Johnson
    California

Harvard beets.

1 Can of beets cut into small strips
2 Teaspoons cornstarch.
Salt.
1/4 cup of sugar
3/4 cup of juice off of beets.
1/4 cup mild vinegar

Cook all of above except the beets, until thick and add beets.

Add lump of butter before serving.

Mrs. Edward Everett Lann

Kansas.

Idaho Potato

I met a big potato
In a Washington cafe,
With eyes so large and wondering
And countenance so gay.
The potato said I've met you
Somewhere way out west,
But this I'm free to tell you
These people love me best.
This life is very grandiose
No dirt or soil or mud
For here they call us "Idahos"
And not the lowly spud.

A potato mealy large and fine
You do not appreciate
For you only call us plain old spuds
Out in our own home state.

Recipe –
Wash and bake.

Mrs Compton White
Idaho.

Idaho Potato Piglets

6 Medium potatoes
6 Skinned frankfurters or sausages

Wash and core the potatoes with an apple corer. Stuff meat into Potatoes. Bake in the usual way. The potatoes may be peeled, if desired, and roasted in dripping pan.

← IDAHO
OVEN →

Mrs. H. C. Dworshak,
Idaho

Onion Pie

Cook 2 C. chopped onions in 1 C. butter for 20 minutes. Do not let the onions brown. Take from fire and cool. Stir in beaten yolks of 6 eggs, ½ C. cream, salt + peper, 1 C white wine and 6 beaten egg whites. Mix in each ingredient slowly and carefully.

Line pie plate with rich pastry.

Pour in mixture and bake for ½ hour in a moderate oven.

The filling should be more than 2 inches deep. No top crust.

To be served hot or cold with salad.

Chase Going Woodhouse
Connecticut

Spanish Peas

1 can small English peas
1 can tomato paste (no points)
1 cup finely chopped onions
1/2 cup chopped green peppers
1/2 Chopped celery
Margarine size of an egg or cooking oil.

Saute onions, pepper and celery in margarine or oil for 10 minutes.
Drain peas and add to this mixture.
Empty can of tomato paste and one can of water to peas and vegetables.
Pour this mixture into a buttered pyrex dish, cover with bread crumbs, and bake in moderate oven about 30 minutes.

Mrs. Pete Jarman - Alabama -

Stuffed Peppers.

Cut slices from top of 6 small green peppers. Remove seeds & parboil 5 minutes. Combine 3 tablespoons minute tapioca, 1 teaspoon salt, 1/8 teaspoon pepper, 1 tablespoon minced onion, 2 cups ground cooked meat, and 1½ cups canned tomatoes; fill peppers with mixture and sprinkle with crumbs. Set upright in baking dish. Bake in hot oven (450° F.) 30 minutes, basting frequently. Serve hot.

Mrs. J. P. Buchanan, Jr.
Texas.

Sunshine Carrots

1 orange rind
1 bunch Carrots
3/4 C. Sugar
2 T butter
1/3 C. Water

Cut the orange rind & scraped carrots into long, narrow pieces similar to shoe string potatoes.

Cook carrots in boiling salty water until tender, drain excess water and season with butter.

Cover orange rind with cold water, bring to a boil, let boil one minute, drain and repeat 3 times.

Prepare a thick syrup with sugar + 1/3 c water. Let orange rind simmer in the syrup about 45 min. or an hour. Add cooked carrots to orange rind and simmer 15 minutes longer. Serve hot as a vegetable.

Mrs. John J. Sparkman
Alabama

Sweet Potato Baskets

4 medium sized potatoes
¼ stick of butter
¼ C sweet milk
3 T. brown sugar
1 C. crushed pineapple
½ tsp. salt
1 tsp. ground cloves
1 tsp. powdered cinnamon
1 T. vinegar
4 T sherry
Grated rind of 1 lemon
Juice of 1 lemon
Juice of 1 orange
Half orange skins
Grated rind of 1 orange

Cream potatoes together with butter, milk and brown sugar, add other ingredients + mix well. Fill 12 large orange shells. Bake in medium oven 20 or 30 minutes. Place a marshmallow on top of each and brown in oven.

Mrs. John L. McMillan
South Carolina.

Tomatoes Creole

Boil Tomatoes with skins on until tender. Remove skins & place on platter. Cover with following sauce.
1 lb. Brown Sugar
2 green peppers
2 tomatoes
½ cup water
Chop tomatoes & peppers in small pieces & cook with sugar & water until syrupy. Pour over tomatoes & serve piping hot.

Mrs. C. Douglass Buck
Delaware

C. C.
Vegetable Scallop
Serves 8

1½ C. each – cooked peas – corn – tomatoes
    carrots (any cooked vegetable)
1½ C. soft bread crumbs
1 T chopped onion
4 T bacon drippings
¼ tsp. salt – pepper to taste
3 beaten eggs
Put in custard cups or casserole
Bake 45 min. at 350°

Sauce
1 cup milk, 2 T butter or substitute
2 T flour, ¼ tsp. salt, ½ lb. grated cheese
½ tsp. mustard – Cook in double boiler.

Mrs. Harold H. Burton
Ohio.

White House Dish

1 egg plant
1 can tomatoes
seasoning
2 green peppers
1 onion
2 T. butter

Place eggplant, peeled and sliced, in bottom of baking dish; cover with part of tomatoes, green peppers and chopped onion; make several layers of this until dish is filled. On top sprinkle seasoning and two T. butter. Cover and bake 45 minutes. This dish is especially palatable with steak or roast.

Mrs. Wesley E. Disney
Oklahoma.

NOTES

For Yours From Us

I.

O here's a book in which to look
    for something good to eat,
For pies to bake; for cookies and cake;
    for a very special treat;
For pickles in spice; for everything nice;
    for waffles, biscuits, and jam;
For apple sauce, and casseroles, and
    dumplings, and roast lamb.

II.

This book's for you, by Bess and Sue,
    by Emily, Peggy, Jane,
By Selma, Eleanor, Alice, Georgia,
    from Idaho to Maine,
By Gertrude, Frances, Dorcas, Betty,
    Helen, Mildred, Anne,
From Illinois to Mississippi and
    to Michigan,
By Dorothy, Martha, Margaret, Mary,
    Mabel, Myrtle, Kate,
By gals from Colorado, Texas, and
    from Washington state,
By Agnes, Emmy, Daisy, Hazel,
    Maureen and Sally and Bella,
By Alma, Louisa, Lillian, Miriam,
    Ruth, and little Nell,

By Dorris, Rachel, Henrietta, Marion,
    Prue, Louella,
By Elizabeth, Ida, Olga, Julia, Florence,
    Faye and Stella,
By Violet, Esther, Edna, Nancy, Winifred,
    Twila, Jessie,
By Clara, Jean, and Joan and May
    and Edith, Chase and Glessie.
These recipes we hope will please
    from New York and Tennessee,
From Nevada and New Jersey and
    Washington D. C.

III.

From Alaska, Alabama, Arizona,
    Arkansas,
Wyoming, West Virginia, Wisconsin,
    and Utah,
Hawaii, ole Virginny, Iowa, and
    Delaware,
From Florida, Connecticut, New
    Hampshire, everywhere,
Oregon, North Carolina, Georgia, Louisiana,
Missouri, Massachusetts, Maryland,
    and big Montana,
Nebraska, South Carolina, Oklahoma,
    North Dakota,
From Indiana, from Rhode Island, and
    from Minnesota,
South Dakota, Pennsylvania, Vermont
    and O-hi-O,

California, Kentucky, Kansas, and New Mexico!
IV.

Yes, here's a book in which to look
    for something good to cook,
It's crammed chuck full of fine ad-
    vice in every single nook!
Yes, here's good cheer throughout the year
    and throughout the country wide,
Designed for the seasoned chef as well
    as the inexperienced bride!
Three cheers for you, three cheers for us,
    three cheers for the gay and the good,
Three cheers for all these recipes
    of rich and luscious food!
We hope you'll find them useful
    every minute of your lives,
Compiled by the Congressional Club, by
    House and Senate wives!
        — Mrs. Hal Holmes.
          Washington.

NOTES

Household Hints

Household Hints

Did you know that a piece of Alum in the silver drawer helps to prevent tarnish?

Tarnish on silver that has been put away for a long time can be removed by soaking in potato water for about 2 hours.

Equal parts of flour and salt moistened with vinegar will clean brass.

To clean Copper use a weak ammonia solution.

Camphorated oil will remove white stains and rings on furniture.

For Coffee, tea, cocoa, or fruit stains, pour boiling water through the stain until it disappears.

10 pounds of Green peas will serve 25 people.

A 13 pound ham will serve 50 people.

1 pound tea will make 100 cups.

1 pound of Coffee will make 40 cups.

3-4 gallons of punch will serve 100 portions.

1 qt. Cream will serve 35-40 people with Cream for Coffee or tea.

1 pound loaf sugar equals 100 Cubes.

1 pound butter makes 36 pats.

1 cup butter   = 1/2 pound
4 cups flour   = 1 pound
2 cups sugar   = 1 pound

Slow oven — — — — 250°F — 325°F

Moderate Oven — — — 350°F — 375°F

Hot Oven — — — — — 400°F — 450°F

Very Hot Oven — — — — 450°F — 500°F

Baking Powder Biscuits
475° for 10-15 minutes

Ginger Bread — — — 350° - 50 min.

Bread (yeast) — — — 375° - 60 min.

Rolls (yeast) — — — 425° - 10-15 m

Rolled Sugar Cookies
425° — — — 8-10 minutes

Other Cookies — —
375° — — — 10-15 min.

When boiling Idaho potatoes start in cold water & when boiling old potatoes add 1 T. vinegar to 1 quart water to whiten the potatoes.

To beat eggs quickly add a pinch of salt.

Heat milk before adding to mashed potatoes.

When powdered sugar becomes lumpy, put it through the flour sieve.

To cut marshmallows use scissors dipped in water.

2 T. of lemon juice added to a cup of sweet milk will sour it at once.

Rub the tip of the cream pitcher with a little butter to prevent cream from running down the outside.

To test baked custard insert a knife, if it comes out clean the custard is done.

Never boil tea or coffee after they are made.

NOTES

NOTES

NOTES

Notes

Index

Name	State	Page
Adams, Mrs. Sherman	N.H.	45, 46
Andersen, Mrs. H. Carl	Minn.	55
Anderson, Mrs. Clinton P.	N.M.	86
Andresen, Mrs. August H.	Minn.	91, 238
Angell, Mrs. Homer D.	Ore.	305
Arnold, Mrs. S. Wat	Mo.	262
Baer, Mrs. John M.	N.D.	109, 327
Barrett, Mrs. Frank A.	Wyo.	296, 312
Bender, Mrs. George H.	O.	83
Bishop, Mrs. C.W.	Ill.	70
Bland, Mrs. Oscar E.	Ind.	273
Bland, Mrs. S. Otis	Va.	309, 328
Bolton, Hon. Frances P.	O.	331
Bonner, Mrs. Herbert C.	N.C.	58, 140
Boren, Mrs. Lyle H.	Okla.	270
Bradley, Mrs. Fred	Mich.	190
Brehm, Mrs. Walter E.	O.	77, 209
Brewster, Mrs. Owen	Me.	251
Brown, Mrs. Clarence J.	O.	73
Buchanan, Mrs. James P.	Tex.	60, 80
Buchanan, Mrs. James P. Jr.	Tex.	129, 374
Buck, Mrs. C. Douglass	Del.	342, 364, 377
Buck, Mrs. Ellsworth B.	N.Y.	229
Buffett, Mrs. Howard H.	Nebr.	22
Burgin, Mrs. William O.	N.C.	11, 237
Burke, Mrs. Edward R.	Nebr.	104, 346

Name	State	Page
Burton, Mrs. Harold	O.	343, 378
Bushfield, Mrs. Harlan J.	S.D.	147, 221
Cannon, Mrs. Clarence	Mo.	74, 81
Carlson, Mrs. Frank	Kan.	136, 253
Carter, Mrs. Albert E.	Calif.	76, 240
Church, Mrs. Ralph E.	Ill.	323
Clason, Mrs. Charles R.	Mass.	313, 315
Clements, Miss Mary Park	Ga.	130
Cole, Mrs. Albert M.	Kan.	36
Cole, Miss Mary Barbara	Mo.	75, 280
Cole, Mrs. William C.	Mo.	256
Cole, Mrs. W. Sterling	N.Y.	260, 294
Cox, Mrs. Eugene E.	Ga.	155
Curtis, Mrs. Carl T.	Nebr.	274, 367
Dale, Mrs. Porter H.	Vt.	148
Daughton, Mrs. Ralph Hunter	Va.	225
Davis, Mrs. Clifford	Tenn.	204, 223
Dewey, Mrs. Charles S.	Ill.	218, 332
Dilweg, Mrs. LaVern R.	Wis.	197
Dirksen, Mrs. Everett M.	Ill.	96, 105
Disney, Mrs. Wesley E.	Okla.	379
Dolliver, Mrs. James I.	Ia.	101
Dondero, Mrs. George A.	Mich.	216, 329
Douglas, Hon. Helen Gahagan	Calif.	286
Dworshak, Mrs. Henry C.	Idaho	43, 371
Ellender, Mrs. Allen J.	La.	182
Ellsworth, Mrs. Harris	Ore.	65
Engel, Mrs. Albert J.	Mich.	87
Ervin, Mrs. Joseph W.	N.C.	267
Farrington, Mrs. Joseph R.	Hawaii	14, 344
Fernandez, Mrs. Antonio M.	N.M.	71, 246
Fisher, Mrs. O.C.	Tex.	242, 310
Evins, Mrs. Joe L. 396	Tenn.	288

Forand, Mrs. Aime J.	R.I.	203,349
Gann, Mrs. Edward Everett	Kan.	17, 57, 232, 369
Garrett, Mrs. Finis	Tenn.	41
George, Mrs. Walter F.	Ga.	35
Gillette, Mrs. Wilson D.	Pa.	143, 175
Gillie, Mrs. George W.	Ind.	59, 275
Goodwin, Mrs. Angier L.	Mass.	193
Gordon, Mrs. Thomas S.	Ill.	53, 107
Grant, Mrs. George M.	Ala.	126, 198
Griffiths, Mrs. P.W.	O.	139
Gwinn, Mrs. Ralph W.	N.Y.	184
Hale, Mrs. Robert	Me.	178
Hancock, Mrs. Clarence E.	N.Y.	9, 230
Harter, Mrs. Dow W.	O.	132, 291, 341
Hawkes, Mrs. Albert W.	N.J.	306, 347
Hedrick, Mrs. Erland H.	W. Va.	112
Heidinger, Mrs. James V.	Ill.	98
Hendricks, Mrs. Joe	Fla.	10, 128
Herbert, Mrs. Joseph A., Jr.	N.D.	271
Herter, Mrs. Christian A.	Mass.	358
Heselton, Mrs. John W.	Mass.	44, 245
Hess, Mrs. William E.	O.	199, 321
Hill, Mrs. William S.	Colo.	15, 125
Hoeven, Mrs. Charles B.	Ia.	89
Holifield, Mrs. Chet	Calif.	100, 236
Holmes, Mrs. Hal	Wash.	124, 217, 295
Hook, Mrs. Frank E.	Mich.	99, 187
Horan, Mrs. Walt	Wash.	19, 239
Izac, Mrs. Edouard Victor	Calif.	241, 326
Jarman, Mrs. Pete	Ala.	355, 373

Name	State	Page
Jennings, Mrs. John Jr.	Tenn.	183
Johnson, Mrs. Jed	Okla	122,330
Johnson, Mrs. J. Leroy	Calif.	200,368
Johnson, Mrs. Noble J.	Ind.	94
Judd, Mrs. Walter H.	Minn.	23,228
Kearney, Mrs. Bernard W.	N.Y.	115
Kefauver, Mrs. Estes	Tenn.	151,174
Kelly, Mrs. Augustine B.	Pa.	293,300
Kilday, Mrs. Paul J.	Tex.	226,318
Kinzer, Mrs. J. Roland	Pa	261
Kopplemann, Mrs. Herman P.	Conn.	249
LaFollette, Mrs. Charles M.	Ind.	131,317
Latta, Mrs. Olga M.	Ky.	95,134
Lea, Mrs. Clarence F.	Calif.	192
LeCompte, Mrs. Karl M.	Ia.	102,311
LeFevre, Mrs. Jay	N.Y.	292
Lemke, Mrs. William	N.D.	152,282
Lewis, Mrs. Earl R.	O.	279
Link, Mrs. William W.	Ill.	79,257
McCowen, Mrs. Edward O.	O.	116
McGregor, Mrs. J. Harry	O.	90,227
McLaughlin, Mrs. Charles F.	Nebr.	37,88
McMillan, Mrs. John L.	S.C.	376
McMillen, Mrs. Rolla C.	Ill.	176
Mahon, Mrs. George H.	Tex.	283
Mansfield, Mrs. Mike	Mont.	219,333
Martin, Mrs. Thomas E.	Ia.	201,285
Michener, Mrs. Earl C.	Mich.	177
Morrison, Mrs. Martin A.	Ind.	25
Morse, Mrs. Wayne	Ore.	21,263

Name	State	Pages
Mundt, Mrs. Karl E.	S.D.	207
Murray, Mrs. Reid F.	Wis.	32
Newton, Mrs. Cleveland A.	Mo.	92
Norrell, Mrs. W. F.	Ark.	186
O'Brien, Mrs. Thomas J.	Ill.	113, 234
O'Neal, Mrs. Emmet	Ky.	50, 314
Outland, Mrs. George E.	Calif.	146, 334
Pace, Mrs. Stephen	Ga.	34, 208
Patman, Mrs. Wright	Tex.	157
Patrick, Mrs. Luther	Ala.	307, 320
Peterson, Mrs. Hugh	Ga.	142, 366
Phillips, Mrs. John	Calif.	135
Plumley, Mrs. Charles A.	Vt.	235, 335
Polk, Mrs. James G.	O.	222
Poulson, Mrs. Norris	Calif.	252, 362
Quick, Mrs. Charles E.	Mich.	18
Ramey, Mrs. Homer A.	O.	231, 259, 339
Ramspeck, Mrs. Robert	Ga.	247, 325
Rankin, Miss Annie Laurie	Miss.	111, 281
Rankin, Mrs. John E.	Miss.	49, 224
Reed, Mrs. Chauncey W.	Ill.	205
Reed, Mrs. Daniel A.	N.Y.	127, 138, 350
Revercomb, Mrs. Chapman	W. Va.	66
Rich, Mrs. Robert F.	Pa.	322, 345
Rizley, Mrs. Ross	Okla.	103, 298
Robertson, Mrs. Edward V.	Wyo.	269
Robinson, Mrs. J. Will	Utah	54, 264
Robsion, Mrs. John M.	Ky.	12, 61
Roe, Mrs. Dudley G.	Md.	51, 118

Rogers, Mrs. Dwight L.	Fla.	- -181,297
Rohrbough, Mrs. Edward Q.	W. Va.	- - -63,284
Roosevelt, Mrs. Franklin D.	N.Y.	- - - -180
Saltonstall, Mrs. Leverett	Mass.	- - -137
Schafer, Mrs. John C.	Wis.	- - -52,244
Schwabe, Mrs. George B.	Okla.	- - -31,154
Schwabe, Mrs. Max	Mo.	- -85,123
Scrivner, Mrs. Errett P.	Kan.	- - - -276
Shafer, Mrs. Paul	Mich.	- - -324,361
Sikes, Mrs. Robert L. F.	Fla.	- - -48, 82
Simpson, Mrs. Sid	Ill.	- - - - -13
Smith, Mrs. Lawrence H.	Wis.	- 16,319,365
Smith, Hon. Margaret Chase	Me.	- 254,308,357
Smith, Mrs. Martin F.	Wash.	- - -62,278
Snyder, Mrs. J. Buell	Pa.	- -258,348
Sparkman, Mrs. John J.	Ala.	- -108,375
Stefan, Mrs. Karl	Nebr.	- -42,206
Stockman, Mrs. Lowell	Ore.	- 299,351,363
Sullivan, Mrs. John B.	Mo.	- - - -214
Sundstrom, Mrs. Frank L.	N.J.	- - -352
Taber, Mrs. John	N.Y.	- - -188
Taft, Mrs. Robert A.	O.	- -149,243
Tarver, Mrs. Malcolm C.	Ga.	- -33,64,117
Taylor, Mrs. Dean P.	N.Y.	179,195,268
Thomas, Mrs. Albert	Tex.	- -196,316
Thomason, Mrs. R. Ewing	Tex	- -255,304
Tolan, Mrs. John H.	Calif.	- -233,250
Truman, Mrs. Harry S.	Mo.	- - -30, 93
Vandenberg, Mrs. Arthur H.	Mich.	- - - -114
Vestal, Mrs. Albert H.	Ind.	- - - -359

Vestal, Miss Vivian	Ind.	153, 359
Voorhis, Mrs. Jerry	Calif.	20, 97
Walters, Mrs. Anderson H.	Pa.	39
Warren, Mrs. Lindsay C.	N.C.	145
Weigester, Mrs. W. Frederick	Kan.	106, 141
Wherry, Mrs. Kenneth S.	Nebr.	189, 248
White, Mrs. Compton I.	Ida.	370
White, Mrs. Dudley A.	O.	47, 72
Whitten, Mrs. Jamie L.	Miss.	158
Whittington, Mrs. William M.	Miss.	191
Wickard, Mrs. Claude R.	Ind.	78
Wickersham, Mrs. Victor	Okla.	277
Wigglesworth, Mrs. Richard B.	Mass.	133
Wiley, Mrs. Alexander	Wis.	272, 360
Wilson, Mrs. Earl	Ind.	156, 185
Winstead, Mrs. Arthur	Miss.	56, 194
Wood, Mrs. John S.	Ga.	24, 340
Woodhouse, Hon. Chase Going	Conn.	372
Woodruff, Mrs. Roy O.	Mich.	144
Zimmerman, Mrs. Orville	Mo.	38, 150
*Murdock, Mrs. John R.	Ariz.	356
Young, Miss Edith L. (Club recipes)		161-170

THE END

www.ingramcontent.com/pod-product-compliance
Lightning Source LLC
Chambersburg PA
CBHW022047160426
43198CB00008B/144